GOD, RELIGION & CIVIL GOVERNANCE

The John Henry Cardinal Newman Lectures

GENERAL EDITOR: *Craig Steven Titus*

The John Henry Cardinal Newman Lecture Series is held under the sponsorship of the Institute for the Psychological Sciences in order to promote an international conversation among the several disciplines that treat the human person. This Washington-based lecture series is held annually, and forthcoming volumes will be published with an eye toward building a body of learned discussion that is catholic both in its breadth of research and in its dialogue with contemporary Catholic thought. The published versions appear under the patronage of St. Catherine of Alexandria in order to demonstrate the conviction of those responsible for the Newman Lecture Series that the human person flourishes only when the Creator of heaven and earth is loved above all things.

The John Henry Cardinal Newman Lectures

VOLUME 6

GOD, RELIGION & CIVIL GOVERNANCE

EDITED BY *Craig Steven Titus*

The Institute for the Psychological Sciences Press
Arlington, Virginia

Distributed by
The Catholic University of America Press
620 Michigan Ave., N.E. / 240 Leahy Hall
Washington, D.C. 20064

The paper used in this publication meets the minimum requirements
of American National Standards for Information Science—
Permanence of Paper for Printed Library Materials, ANSI Z39.48-1984.
∞

Library of Congress Cataloging-in-Publication Data
God, religion, and civil governance / edited by Craig Steven Titus.
pages cm. — (The John Henry Cardinal Newman lectures ; Volume 6)
Includes index.
ISBN 978-0-9773103-9-5 (pbk. : alk. paper)   1. Freedom of religion—
United States.   2. Church and state—United States.   3. Religion and
politics—United States.   I. Titus, Craig Steven, 1959– editor.
BR516.G54 2014
323.44'2—dc23   2014016512

CONTENTS

Acknowledgments   vii

Introduction   1
Craig Steven Titus

1. Freedom of Religion   18
Roger Scruton

2. Religion and State: Some Main Issues
and Sources   35
John Finnis

3. The Eclipse of the Sense of God and Man   67
Livio Melina

4. That "Intelligent Superintending Principle":
The Author of the Rights That Were There
before the Constitution and the Bill of Rights   84
Hadley Arkes

5. On the Moral Purposes of Law and the State:
First Principles and Contemporary Issues   109
Robert P. George

6. "Rights" and Our Essential Nature   128
Daniel N. Robinson

Contributors   145
Index of Names   149
Index of Subjects   151

ACKNOWLEDGMENTS

In the name of the Institute for the Psychological Sciences (Arlington, Virginia), I would like to acknowledge the many actors who contributed to making possible this collection of essays from the 2006–7 John Henry Cardinal Newman Lecture Series. First of all, I would like to recognize the faithful generosity of Gene and Charlotte Zurlo, who have funded the Newman Lecture Series from its inception. Furthermore, because of Dr. John Harvey's benevolent sponsorship, the lectures were held at the Cosmos Club (Washington, D.C.), which has offered a fitting ambiance for genteel discussions. The corporate and personal authorities of the Institute for the Psychological Sciences have warmly encouraged the publication of these lectures. Trevor Lipscombe, director of the Catholic University of America Press, and his staff have contributed their competent and careful aid in bringing this volume to fruition, as have Philip Holthaus (copyeditor) and David Kovacs, Stephanie Balceniuk, and Laura Cusumano (graduate assistants). Finally, I would like to acknowledge the foresight of Professor Daniel N. Robinson, who inspired this series, and the commitment and energy of Dean Emeritus Gladys Sweeney, who mobilized a host of prominent scholars and organized the series and this publication.

GOD, RELIGION & CIVIL GOVERNANCE

.

Craig Steven Titus

INTRODUCTION

Liberty and autonomy are essential to contemporary Western democratic societies. But so is religion. Religious freedom even serves as the most basic liberty that protects our other freedoms and human rights and the common good as well. Recognizing the source of life is of primary importance for human flourishing. But religious freedom cannot be reduced to the freedom to worship the God of the universe. It also includes recognizing the moral structure of the universe and moral principles, such as honor the basic dignity of each human person; respect human life as sacred from conception to natural death; do not directly cooperate in evil; and do not bear false witness. Nonetheless, claims to defend certain individual rights and governmental prerogatives have been used to limit religious and other basic freedoms and rights. Thus, legislation has been established that defends a woman's right to choose over the unborn human being's human right to life.

Christianity has influenced Western civilization's notion of God and religion, as well as its laws and forms of governance. Nonetheless, the effect of secularization and extreme views on the separation of church and state have created new challenges and raised new questions for mankind. Libertarian and fundamentalist claims that either under- or overvalue the practical implications of religion for civil governance trouble the texture of civil society and strike at the very nature of the moral order. The effort to defend moral truth and religion against exaggerated claims of conservatism and progressivism has everything to do with defending the person, marriage, the family, and the nation. It also raises the question about the place of conscientious objection and disobedience of unjust laws.

Effectively, the claims of religion within a pluralistic and permissive political order are of great import. In between extreme forms of collectivism and liberalism and between fundamentalism and relativism, the six authors who contribute to this volume seek to establish a middle ground. This balanced position is constituted by the principles of respect for the Creator, dignity of each human person, support for marriage, and justice for the family and the nation. Questions that lead to identifying such a middle position include the following: How can civil governments defend the prerogative of law, the autonomy of the individual person, and the competing claims of diverse religious communities? Can liberties or rights be coherently thought to be unrestrained? Does relativism or fundamentalism give a viable vision of human flourishing? Does the U.S. Constitution presuppose a structure of objective moral truths? Does the Constitution's First Amendment presuppose that religion is the "first freedom"? The essays in this volume address these questions and other major issues concerning God, religion, and civil governance in a way that offers guidance for a civic culture that seeks both a sure sense of its roots and a level measure for future governance supported by just law, human dignity, and virtuous character.

⁓

Roger Scruton analyzes the major philosophical and historical developments in religious freedom, especially three construals of society that vie for dominance in Western civilization: atheist secularism, militant theocracy, and an intermediate position that would permit and even promote circumscribed religious practices.

James Madison and the other American Founders, having fled religious persecutions, were keen to make the First Amendment of the American Constitution inhibit laws that would either establish religion or prohibit its free exercise. The Founders intended a middle ground that protected both religion and the state in their respective purposes. Although this amendment has served the American experiment well, the free exercise of religion has come to mean something quite different from that intended by the Founders, who sought to separate state from religion, but not to exclude faith from the public domain.

The original intention of the nonestablishment and free-exercise clause was to resist a theocratic correlation of state and Christianity that has, in intolerant periods, produced the persecution of minority groups. In particular, the Founders had in mind the state-supported and state-controlled Church of England of their time. Although the Christian West has seen a redressing of theocratic practices due to constitutional democratic institutions that it has engendered (including its laws and treaties, notably, the European Convention and the Treaties of the European Union), there are still theocratic tendencies in some Judeo-Christian positions. Moreover, whether envisaged or not by the American Founders, at present in the West there is also a real Islamic tendency toward theocracy. Scruton records the claims of Islam that do not pretend to apply only to countries under Islamic law (*Shari'ah*) but also to countries where Muslims abide as a minority.

However, the balance of state and religion is threatened not only by the overextension of Christian and Islamic pretensions. There are secularist readings of the First Amendment and similar European conventions and treatises that would make such documents have an antireligious effect, at times going so far as promoting a type of atheism in the name of freedom of religion and equality for all. A bounding secularism has promoted "the culture of repudiation" that involves the systematic rejection of the Western "cultural and religious inheritance." Rather than inheriting religious freedom, it seeks to censor religion (belief, rites, and community expressions) except those that are most privately exercised and, oddly enough, those of minority groups. As Scruton emphasizes, the effect is that an atheistic approach to secularization has become a type of religion that wields censorship of religion (but mostly majority religion) in the name of religious freedom and equality. This atheistic secularism even has the tendency to censor public expressions and practices of Christianity, while supporting the rights of minority groups. For example, in the name of religious freedom, there is censorship to rational critiques leveled against Islamic practices that are illegal in the West yet carried out in some European countries (such as polygamy, forced marriage, female circumcision, and honor killings). Critiques made of such practices are censored, while Christianity has a hard time—even where it is a majority religion—receiving the respect given to minority religions.

Scruton evaluates the boundary claims concerning religious freedom in rapport with three qualities of any religion: belief, ritual, and community. He highlights the contributions that Christianity (in dialogue with its Jewish roots and the Greek and Roman legal, moral, and intellectual tradition) has made in promoting the well-being of its adherents and society through its teachings, practices, and social impact. Distortions aside, Christianity, as the majority religion of the West, has produced in its legal and political traditions a model of secular authority that effectively promotes a viable vision of religious freedom. In circumscribing religion and distinguishing it from the state, the state and civil society can recognize the majority religion (and its practices, even public ones), while also upholding the religious freedom of minorities. Christianity serves this model well, since it permits religious freedom and even requires it.

~)

In his reflections on religion and state, John Finnis approaches religion, state, and law through philosophical inquiry and historical reflections. He writes as a philosopher of law and political order, as well as an observer of our times. While not entering the domain of properly theological reflections, he works at the same time to uncover biases against transcendent values and reality. He starts by outlining two philosophical arguments for the existence of God (one based on patterns of function that are within reach of personal experience and modern sciences and the other based on the orderliness of things), showing that without such considerations the universe is radically underexplained. In this philosophical consideration of God's nature as intelligent and free and of the possibility and probability of divine revelation (given the nature of the universe), the qualities of intelligence, freedom, and the common good (including human rights) serve as standards for the consistency and lack of coercion that are best used in the public practice and promotion of religion. In these considerations, what is at stake is the legitimacy of religious claims in public debate and the use of coercion.

There are two extreme opposing positions regarding the correlation of religion and state. On the one hand, secularist theories exclude religion from consideration in public. One such theory maintains that religious claims about God and man are unreasonable and should be rejected from the domain of public reason (i.e., politics and education); and this should occur whether religion is understood as in the major religious traditions or as each individual's own conception of meaning and deep concerns about the universe. On the other hand, theocratic theories maintain the right to impose the view of one religion on its adherents and even on nonadherents by force of coherence. In between these two extremes, and in the contemporary culture that lacks consensus about the universe's dependence on God, how does religion play a role in political communities? In addition to political philosophy and historical considerations, the U.S. Constitution's First Amendment's protection of "the free exercise of religion," the European Convention on Human Rights, and the Second Vatican Council's Declaration on Religious Liberty (*Dignitatis Humanae*) offer natural law and positive law arguments about religion and state, in particular about interdictions to the use of coercion in religious belief, expression, and practice. In his "Regensburg Address," Benedict XVI argues that both violence and unreasonableness are contrary not only to God's nature but also to the human good of religion. But more than finding coercive violence unfitting of state or religion, Finnis, quoting *Dignitatis Humanae,* argues that the state, in the name of the temporal common good (and human rights), needs to "recognize and favor the religious life of the citizenry, but must be said to exceed its limits if it presume to direct or inhibit religious acts."[1] But what rights and duties apply to state and citizen in these matters? Aquinas and *Dignitatis Humanae* would limit jurisdiction (and its coercive nature) to external acts that trouble the just and peaceful ordering of the political community. Even though a person has a duty to pursue truth about the ultimate source and finality of the universe, the state can neither rightfully nor effectively compel internal acts, vows, or faith and worship in this line.

This is fine from the part of the state, but what about from the side of religion and the religious person: Is there a right to proclaim any notion of religion? This question is more difficult and delicate in the midst of present religious practices that exercise implicit and explicit forms of coercion. (Here Finnis describes those related to fundamentalist versions of religion, including Christianity and, in some detail, Islam.) First, there is a negative duty "not to coerce religious acts unless these threaten the rights of others, public peace or public morality." However, a second issue concerns whether state governments have a negative duty not to discriminate between religions. These two negative duties are related inasmuch as the state must make certain discriminations concerning acts (and the religious doctrine that promote them), when those religious acts disserve the temporal common good, the rights of others, and public peace. Examples would concern those "who give open or covert or tacit support to the religious doc-

---

1. Second Vatican Council, *Dignitatis Humanae* [Declaration on Religious Liberty], (Vatican City: Libreria Editrice Vaticana, 1965), n. 31.

trines and practices of intimidation"; excluding or expulsing a non-national clergyman (as is approved in the U.K. Equality Act, 2006) would be compatible with the "true right of religious liberty," in Finnis's appraisal.

Lastly, there is the issue of whether the state has a positive duty to encourage religious activities[2] and even to adopt a religion as true, which would mean that it "holds out its moral teaching as a matter of public reason." In discussing the related duties, Finnis argues once again for a via media, between the state that would express the belief that no religion is true and the state that would persecute any religious expressions not consistent with the state-adopted religion. In the middle stands a number of duties that would "recognize and favor religion" that Finnis affirms means true religion (the true religious faith and community).

Livio Melina appraises public morality and modern civilization in terms of the dominant construals of science and technology. He notes that presently modern science and civilization risk eclipsing man from himself. However, the eclipsing of man from himself—that is, the denial of knowledge about human nature—is rooted in the previous eclipsing of the sense of God the Creator from the boundaries of public discourse and culture. The product of these successive eclipses is to use technology and biotechnology without a moral conscience and a sense of human anthropology. If biotechnology's use is not based on a conception of human dignity and the natural rights that there ensue, such applications of science might turn against man.

Modern sciences, ever since Galileo, have tended to progressively employ a fact-salvation dichotomy in order to avoid conflict between the scientific and religious spheres. Autonomous scientific reasoning has been progressively distinguished from religious belief in such a way as to divide the unity of knowledge by opposing public and objective science to subjective and private belief. The progressive sepa-

---

2. See Second Vatican Council, *Dignitatis Humanae*, n. 1.

ration of modern science from moral values and their religious and metaphysical foundations has prepared the way for a continuation of this separation in the applications of technology. Without guidance to determine valid ends and applications, technologies run headlong toward a "posthuman" world. Melina affirms that the rationality of science must depend upon a larger and more founding rationality based in reality (in nature and open to the Creator Logos) or else find itself a mere idealism and constructivism. However, the human sciences per se cannot give a vision of the human person that is adequate to guide itself and biotechnology. While it is imperative to gain a solid conception of human nature in order to guide science and technology, it is impossible that the modern sciences give themselves this knowledge, inasmuch as they employ strictly mathematical (measures) and pragmatic (statistics) calculations, which are not conducive to a larger horizon of human rationality.

Public morality, on the other hand, in modernity has also acquired a constrained notion of rationality. From the seventeenth century on, humanists, led by Dutch lawyer and theologian Hugo Grotius, have sought to employ autonomous reason in order to extract the rules (natural law) that would order social life. However, the basis for this work has been divisive and based on an "impious" hypothesis, as Grotius put it, that God either does not exist or does not intervene in human affairs. This conception of independent reason (as the foundation of public order) involves a methodological exclusion of religion from public conscience and society. It has promoted a secularization that confines belief in God to the private realm. At the same time, it has served to detach individuals from their tradition and the communities that feed their moral certainties. Moreover, its reductionist and antimetaphysical perspectives claim that morality is no more than emotions or subjective decisions. The first approaches to modern formalism that would base morality on pure reason might not have intended to change the content of Christian morality—but rather to assure its practical application (by rational standards). However, without employing a religious worldview (and Christian revelation) to support Christian values and pressed in by a radically secularized pluralistic context, the Christian finds it difficult to hold these values with any firmness. Such is the case for holding to the values of human "dignity" and "common good."

Blaise Pascal (1623–62) ventured a practical response to atheist friends and to the secularization of his day. Instead of an "impious" hypothesis that effectively excludes God in social life (even for the believer), he proposes a practical approach that involves conducting life as if God existed (*veluti si Deus daretur; even for the nonbeliever*). Benedict XVI has gone ever further in his call to admit of the intrinsic unity that keeps theology, philosophy, and the sciences together. This perspective "opens the spaces of rationality wider."[3] It seeks both to overcome the effect of a narrow vision of science (and the unilateralism of a single method) and to promote openness to reality. Thus, these different methods do not mean that one method is irrational as perceived from another, nor that a rational method could assume or conclude with consistency that it has a basis in irrationality (or that reality is irrational). Moreover, it posits a human participation in reason (Logos), a participation that can draw from these different perspectives. On the contrary, materialistic reductionism renders science vulnerable to manipulation. The simple recognition that a certain use of technology has wrought ecological damage calls upon a rationality of another dimension that would also consider justice, care, forgiveness, love, and so on, and these in their profoundest roots, in the Creator Logos. The moral rationality of public life is upheld in the "hypothesis" or wager of God. In particular, the human dignity of each person and the common good, which are rooted in the sacredness of life and given by God, provide irreducible standards for public social life.

3. Benedict XVI, *Address to the Participants of the IV National Convention of the Italian Church,* Verona (Vatican City: Libreria Editrice Vaticana, October 19, 2006). See also his *Address to the University of Regensburg* (Vatican City: Libreria Editrice Vaticana, September 12, 2006) and his *Address on the Occasion of the 10th Anniversary of "Fides et ratio"* (Vatican City: Libreria Editrice Vaticana, October 16, 2008).

Hadley Arkes examines the question of human rights and their foundations in the context of the American Constitution and Bill of Rights. The Founders, notably James Wilson and Alexander Hamilton, voiced concerns that a bill of rights (added to the Constitution) might misinstruct Americans about the ground of these rights and whether they are simply rights of positive law. When looking at the connection of those rights included in the Bill of Rights (and others that are not included), one might ask: Is any right more central or fundamental than the others? Is it the right to free speech or to bear arms? Moreover, is the juridical perspective on such rights as a restraint on the government (e.g., in the case of silencing critics) adequate to understand their exercise? For example, could a right to free speech be intelligible without access to a basis (the principles of judgment) to distinguish rightful and wrongful speech? Are the enumerated rights of the Constitution's Bill of Rights, for example, easily misconstrued if not understood in their larger grounding? There is the view that these rights are simply positive rights (positive law) as decreed by human institutions. As with the American Civil Liberties Union, there are those who claim that liberty should be unrestrained, seemingly holding that there is no moral truth or ground on which to distinguish legitimate versus illegitimate speech.

Arkes examines the interrelation of law, rights, and moral judgments in order to answer these questions and to determine whether rights can stand without some deeper foundation. He illustrates—through the writings of the Founders—that "the First Amendment presupposes a structure of objective moral truths." Concerning the correlation of the basic rights, furthermore, it is not the right to free speech or the right to bear arms or the right to liberty in sexual matters (and the related right to order an abortion) that are most vital for a regime of freedom. Rather, based on the First Amendment and the Constitution itself, Arkes reminds us of the case for recognizing religion as the "first freedom." In this regard, James Madison positively correlates religion and constitutional order. In that vision of religion, the duty owed to the Creator influences also obligations relating to the laws of human nature, including the use of the human capacity to act morally and to reflect on the origin of all things. The idea of religion is based on the belief in the existence of a Creator who is the author of moral laws, which are not only outside of ourselves and prior to any human civil constitution, but their obligation precedes that pertaining to civil society and positive law. On this basis, the acquisition of a moral sense, to recognize and embody the obligation to respect laws, is the basis for subjects of God and citizens of state. This conception of religion involves more than tolerance, but rather establishes a limit on the reach of political authority.

In basic structure, the fitting ordering of state and each human person has a similarity. Government restrained by just law parallels a human being with self-control (virtuous character). Each involves a type of constitutional rule that cannot claim the "right to do wrong." Each is stronger for it. Each makes reference to a source of ordering (a body of moral truths that command respect) that is beyond itself and that serves as a starting point for moral growth and for civil governance. For each, the moral law (and the author of that law) precedes positive law and civil society.

In this view (James Wilson) the Constitution and the Bill of Rights did not create rights but rather venture to secure the rights possessed by nature. The view of the Federalists (such as Hamilton and Wilson) thus rejects the constructivist moral understanding of Hobbes (expressed in the *Leviathan,* 1651). As Hamilton wrote in "The Farmer Refuted" (1775), this view supposes "an intelligent superintending principle, who ... has constituted an eternal and immutable law, which is indispensibly, obligatory upon all mankind, prior to any human institution whatever." This is a view of a cosmos with a moral structure.

Because the Federalists held that there were natural rights and objective principles of right and wrong, Wilson could make the argument that American law began by incorporating a principle of revolution (in the face of tyranny) and correction (in the face of any unjust law). While contrary to Locke or Blackstone, this idea is not foreign to natural right theorists.

There is moreover the question of the ground for affirming the intrinsic dignity and value of human beings. The language of dignity, sanctity, and rights has persisted, but the sources of that language, especially the deepest language of religious sources, have been resisted by the courts and lost to many, even those who are religious. In the absence of the affirmation that God underwrites unalienable, natural rights, there have been different attempts to justify the language and claims thereto. Arkes demonstrates why self-referential and constructivist accounts are inadequate. In providing a stable foundation for human dignity and natural rights, Arkes argues that theories of the natural law (as rooted in divine law) and of human nature (as created in the image of God) can be supported by reason (without revelation). Furthermore, sanctity is found in the rational foundation for belief in divinity (as John Paul II explains in *Fides et Ratio,* n. 36) and in the religious sense that humans possess. At the same time, these latter theories provide a basis for understanding the principled reasoning needed for the moral agent and for civil governance. Thus, a fitting understanding of the particular laws and rights comes only in seeing both their interconnections and the larger design of which they are but parts. That we can account for positive rights and law only by understanding the nature of human beings, whose special intellectual capacities—including the gift of reason—are understood as participating in laws outside human beings. This is understood as the image of God, which refers to the divine Creator who bestows basic sanctity, dignity, and rights on all human beings equally.

≈)

Robert P. George addresses the moral purposes of law and the state by investigating the boundaries of the powers, responsibilities, and competencies of civil government as well as those of citizens and private institutions. In so doing, he treats the first principles of law and the state as well as some contemporary issues, notably, the dignity of human life, the nature and effects of abortion and cloning, and conceptions of marriage and nonconjugal partnerships.

In general, government has a primary responsibility to defend the nation, protect people from assaults, and maintain public order. Nonetheless, it has a subsidiary responsibility to support the work of families, religious communities, and civil institutions whose primary responsibility is to form moral citizens that mutually care for and respect each other. In regard to these responsibilities, diverse conceptions of liberty and autonomy—both legally protected and privately employed—make a difference in the protection of public health, safety, and morals and in the advancement of the general welfare (or common good).

Against practices of government usurpation, political morality requires a government not merely to respect autonomous practices in familial, religious, and other nongovernmental spheres, but to favor certain liberties and practices (in the nongovernmental sphere) for the stake of the common good. The exact nature of the limits of government and the liberties of nongovernmental instances are at issue. George levels critiques against extreme forms of collectivism and liberalism, while supporting the regulation of free markets (against exploitation) and the import of moral truths (such as those expressed in the Declaration of Independence: "that all men are created equal, that they are endowed by their Creator with certain unalienable rights, and among these are life, liberty, and the pursuit of happiness"). In this middle ground of the American Founders' liberalism, it is erroneous to suppose that the principles of limited government and of basic rights spring from a denial either of moral truth or of the need for the law and the state to act from judgments of moral truth. The affirmation that human beings possess an equal dignity simply by their humanity underscores the political and ethical foundation of American liberalism. These principles, based in natural law and biblical teaching, serve furthermore the domain of practical politics, but not without further moral reflection and argument. Critical issues such as "abortion, embryo-destructive stem-cell research, euthanasia, cloning, and homosexual marriage" cannot be well addressed without citizens and statesmen engaging moral arguments "lovingly and civilly, but also passionately and with determination." The need to make the moral case, however, does not mean that there is no moral truth about the nature of abortion or of marriage; rather, it means that the nature of these truths must be defended against misreading. The truth of the dignity and the sanctity of each human being, demands, for example, that every member of humanity be respected and protected "irrespective not merely of race, sex, and ethnicity, but also of age, size, location, stage of development, and condition of dependency." The protection of innocent human life is the most fundamental moral purpose of government. But abortion, the destruction of human embryos ("spare" or cloned for experimental purposes), and fetal farming also desecrate the moral proposition that all are created equal.

George discusses strategies of the pro-life movement at juridical, political, and popular levels, but also those of the pro-marriage and family movement. Strong families, based on stable marriages, serve "health, education, and welfare" functions in a way that the state cannot. Because of this subsidiary responsibility, a limited-government approach will reject the privatization of marriage (i.e., the reconstrual of marriage) and back government support for stable marriages and a marriage culture. Using data about family health and the influence of unilateral divorce legislation (and nonmarital sexual cohabitation), George supports the conjugal conception of marriage as "the union of one man and one woman pledged to permanence and fidelity and committed to caring for children who come as the fruit of their matrimonial union." He argues that the acceptance of the idea that people of the same sex could marry not only undercuts key features of marriage, but would also lead to polyamory. (Since, if love were the only principle, what could prevent three or more partners from marrying?) Moreover, if same-sex marriages become accepted nationwide, it is foreseeable that the principle of nondiscrimination would be used against private and religious institutions that are committed to a conjugal conception of marriage.

On the contrary, the defense of marriage requires understanding of what marriage is (as a matter of moral truth). In order to correct a free-standing use of a minimalist and overly inclusive reading of the principle "love makes the family," a debate that advances an articulate vision of the conjugal conception of marriage is required. Moreover, there is a dire need to renew the marriage culture (with legal reforms, better marriage preparation, and training for those who work to support troubled marriages). There is also the need for concerted national efforts to right the judgments of liberal activist judges who tend to usurp democratic legislative authority by radically redefining marriage. George outlines other solutions, such as legislating for domestic partnerships that would meet the expectations of financially interdependent persons who are not married (without causing confusion about conjugal relationships). In sum, the defense of marriage and the protection of life, far from being side issues for a democratic government, are at the heart of the moral purposes of law and the state.

In defending a robust notion of essential human nature, Daniel Robinson establishes a foundation for basic human rights and duties. Such an erudite vision underscores the rule of law and the end of human flourishing. Respect for the basic needs of individuals, in the midst of modern pluralism, requires a robust notion of duty. Indeed, there are troubling yet all too common practices that do not respect human dignity, for example, female genital mutilation, forced organ removal, abortion, and war crimes, to name a few. At present, as during the Enlightenment of Montesquieu, plurality and diversity present both a cause for celebration and a cause for alarm. Diversity has its limits. The protean character of human nature is the basis for determining those limits and what is fit for humankind. Nonetheless, the essential character of human nature is challenged by the relativist use of evolutionary notions. Such challenges make us wonder: What would become of international rights courts or the rule of law if there were no essentialist notion of human nature, rights, and duty?

John Locke and Aristotle speak to the issue. Locke provides metaphysical support for understanding the continuity of personal identity in his *Two Treatises of Government* (1690). He grounds the real essence and moral judgment in the law of nature and the will of God. Aristotle, for his part, offers defense for an essentialist understanding of human nature. Man is a rational animal who employs intellectual deliberation in his social and political life. Aristotle comes to conclude that human beings, by their essential nature, need law and are fit to employ law for the common good of the polis.

Robinson also calls on research concerning "psychological essentialism" to illustrate the common human disposition to describe and understand nature as having essences. He showcases pragmatic and sociobiological explanations (apart from metaphysical ones). From an early age, humans perceive and relate to the world in essentialist terms. This way of thinking has survival advantages. With the essence of a thing in mind, both children and adults are able to anticipate events that are not yet observed. The cognitive function of "essentializing" induces from the thing not only its essence but also how it might act and interact with a human person. This cognitive disposition supports classifying objects according to their effects even without fully understanding the causal chain involved in each effect. This judgment, based on an understanding of essences, is not superstition or ignorance but a feature of our capacity for prediscursive evaluations rooted in experiences of things essentially alike. The perception and understanding of man as essentially rational and social suggests precisely that certain types of activity will lead not only to survival but even to a type of flourishing that is fit for subjects like us.

Morality and the rule of law require a minimal capacity for free and responsible agency, as well as the human strengths and vulnerability that are required to rule and to be ruled by law. Vulnerability and need serve as the basis for rights, while powers and capacities serve as the basis for duties. On the one hand, rights protect the person from the vulnerabilities and needs that match with essential features, such as being capable of pain and suffering, misery and loss. On the other hand, duties are constituted by the powers and capacities to act and to meet these needs. Such powers are the grounds for basic duties that people must assume in due time. The fact that people do not exercise these powers when young, disabled, or aged discredits neither the reality of the corresponding duties nor the basic rights of such individuals. For example, it is the essential nature of the person and its vulnerability to being enslaved or killed that is the ground for the human right to freedom or to life. The strength of those in places of power and authority grounds their duty to respect human freedom and life. No authority can revoke basic human rights, since they are grounded in the ontology of the person instead of being attributed nominally or constructed by family, community, or state. They are possessed rather than given. They are possessed even when one traverses borders. They are possessed even when they have not been claimed by the concerned persons.

one

Roger Scruton

FREEDOM OF RELIGION

Where the spirit of the Lord is, there is liberty.

2 Cor. 3:17

The First Amendment to the American Constitution tells us that Congress shall "make no law respecting an establishment of religion or prohibiting the free exercise thereof." Religious freedom is listed among the Human Rights guaranteed by the United Nations Declaration: a freedom added (Article 18) at the request of the Lebanese delegate, Charles Malik, who had the interests of Christians in the Islamic countries in mind. Religious freedom is also guaranteed by the European Convention and the Treaties of the European Union. Churches of every denomination emphasize that we are as free to leave them as we are to join them, and there is plenty of evidence that this is so.

Even the Koran tells us that "there shall be no compulsion [*ikrah*] in religion" (Koran 2.256). It seems that there is universal agreement that religious freedom is among the highest aims of human kind, and one that somehow stands above the thing that it makes possible— namely, freely adopted faith.

Look at things more closely, however, and you will see how very deceptive that interpretation is. Islam, while asserting that no-one shall be compelled to embrace the faith, seems to accept that every Muslim can be compelled to retain it. It is true that, while the Koran makes frequent reference to God's displeasure at apostasy, it is possible to read the relevant passages as stopping short of advocating punishment for apostasy here below. (See 2.217; 3.86–91; 4.115; 5.54; 6.71; 16.106–7.) However, leading authorities, including al-Shafi'i, Baydawi, and Maududi, argue that the Koran authorizes and indeed commands such punishment, and according to the *Shari'ah* apostasy is punishable by death. Moreover, even if Christians and Jews, as "people of the book," are not to be compelled to renounce their faith, the rules laid down for treating them (i.e., as *dhimmi,* or people "protected by treaty") have been singularly harsh in intention. Copts are still second-class citizens in Egypt, as are Christians in Pakistan. And nowhere in the Muslim world are non-Muslims permitted to make converts. As for pagans, atheists, Buddhists, and Hindus, Islam has tolerated them only when obliged by their numbers and their power, and has no clear revelation that forbids their destruction should they refuse to convert.

Nor should we neglect the equal and opposite distortion of the idea of religious freedom that has emerged in Christian countries, and especially here in America. When the Founding Fathers, under the influence of James Madison, inserted the "no establishment" clause into the Constitution it was not because they wished people to cease acknowledging their religion in public life. The Founders were Christians, who wished to retain and to propagate their faith, but who were also acutely aware of the religious oppressions of Europe, from which their ancestors had fled to the New World in order freely to practice their faith. The Founders wanted to separate state from church, not to exclude faith from public life. And they wanted free churches, answerable to their congregations and not to lawmakers. The Established Church of England was to them repugnant less as an attempt to impose Christianity than as a symbol of royal power and its intrusion into every sphere of social life. Moreover the "no establishment" clause was meant as a limitation on the powers of *Congress,* and not on the powers of the individual states. The Founders surely did not intend the clause to authorize Congress to intrude on the State of Massachusetts, for example, which at the time had an absolute ban against Roman Catholicism—a ban that the federal government made no effort to lift.

Yet that is not how the "no establishment" clause is interpreted today. It is invoked as an absolute command against religion in the public arena throughout the Union, and as authority for the radical secularization of all social institutions that depend upon the state, or which exercise an authority that derives from the state. It has been regarded as a violation of the "no establishment" clause that a court should display the Ten Commandments, or that public schools should begin the day with prayers. Such decisions do not convey a desire to protect religious freedom, but a desire to marginalize religion—indeed, to deprive religion of the place that it naturally demands in the public life of a Christian nation. Nobody was forcing children to take part in the public prayers at school, or forcing anyone to genuflect before the Ten Commandments in the courtroom. Yet there are currents of opinion in America that not only take offense at school prayers and doctrinal icons, but that believe that it is part of the spirit of democratic freedom to forbid them. Religion, for such people, is not just a private affair: it is something to be *privatized,* to be confined within the home like some shameful habit that cannot be displayed in public.

It might reasonably be objected that religious freedom, so defined, is actually a forbidding of religion, since it removes the freedom to practice religion in the way that faith demands: in other words, the first part of the "no establishment" clause, strictly interpreted, enters into conflict with the second. The principal demand that the Christian religion makes of its adherents is that they should bear witness to the faith in their life and work, and that they should invite others to join them in worship and prayer. If those things are forbidden, then it is difficult to see that American citizens really are free to be Christians. I think this point bears heavily on the situation of teachers in public schools, many of whom find themselves in the position of being the sole educative influence on children who are not going to obtain the good news of their salvation from any other source.

The vehemence with which the marginalization of religion has been pursued in the name of the "no establishment" clause is remarkable, and suggests that there is a strong antireligious animus at work. Indeed, contemporary moves toward secularization have a decidedly ambiguous character. On the one hand, there is the desire to affirm the Western tradition of secular authority against Islamic theocracy— a worthy desire that surely unites all of us against a very real threat. On the other hand, there is a kind of proselytising anticlericalism, not to say atheism, that turns on our Christian inheritance as though it were an equal threat to our liberties and an equal insult to our legal and political settlement. Moreover, it is precisely the status of Christianity as a majority religion that attracts this kind of attack. Jews, Zoroastrians, Hindus, and even Muslims are given space for their religious needs in public institutions where Christians are forbidden to gather in prayer.

Nor is this phenomenon confined to America. In Britain many state schools will celebrate the Hindu Diwali and the Muslim 'Eid, but resolutely refuse to acknowledge Christmas, or even to refer to Christmas by its proper name, preferring to describe it as the "holiday season," wishing their children "Happy Holidays" as they leave the school for the last time before the festival. Such practices are justified in the name of religious freedom. "We want to leave children free to practice whichever religion they or their parents prefer," say the officials. "It is not for us to impose any particular faith." But the only target of this self-censorship is Christianity, which is driven from public life precisely because of its status as the traditional religion and institution-building force of Western civilization. The Christian religion is being effectively censored out at the very moment when radical Islam wishes to exterminate it; and it is being censored in the name of religious freedom. This is an instance of something that I have called "the culture of repudiation": by which I mean the systematic rejection of the cultural and religious inheritance on which our societies have hitherto depended. In other words, a systematic refusal to inherit.

Now it is difficult to confront this culture of repudiation directly: it is the product of doubts and resentments that lie too deeply implanted in the collective psyche. But we can at least examine what religious freedom is or ought to be, and its relation to the political order with which we are familiar. And in doing so we can perhaps prepare ourselves with an answer to the Islamists, when they tell us that religious freedom is most clearly manifest in the moment when we renounce it and submit to the will of God—after which we are no longer free. This one-way religious freedom of the Muslims, compared to the two-way freedom that we enjoy in the West, is only doubtfully described as freedom, since it replaces freedom with compulsion just as soon as the choice has been made. For us, freedom is a condition that endures, even after our most fundamental choices. That is part of what Cardinal Newman meant by "the grammar of assent"—that our assent is always a free act of the intellect, that cannot be compelled from outside.

Nevertheless, even in Christian cultures, religious freedom is not the clear-cut objective that we might be tempted to assume. Faith involves definite obligations, as well as a commitment to a precise moral code. A law that forbids those obligations or violates that moral code is not one that the believer can obey. A democrat might believe that the constitution and procedures of his country confer legitimacy on its laws. But those laws might still contravene his religious code, and place him under a duty of disobedience.

It is necessary, however, to make some distinctions. A law might authorize conduct that faith forbids, without imposing that conduct on the believer. Such a law, it seems to me, is not a threat to religious freedom. For example, laws permitting abortion and homosexual conduct, which violate the religiously derived moral code of Catholics, do not oblige Catholics to do anything that their faith forbids, or to refrain from doing anything that their faith commands. Catholics may regret these laws, but they are not oppressed by them. On the other hand, laws forbidding discrimination may, in certain cases, violate religious scruples. A law forbidding discrimination against homosexuals may be used to force people to employ homosexuals in some office that religion forbids to them. And there is a definite and growing tension between the laws enforcing gender equality and the position of the Catholic Church, which regards only men as qualified for priesthood.

There is a further dimension to all this, and it goes to the heart of what political freedom means. A Washington-based pressure group is currently campaigning to remove state funding from a marriage guidance network that uses the Bible as a leading source. The group argues that by funding this network, the state violates the "no establishment" clause. You can see how the argument goes, and the kind of plausibility that it might achieve. What is important, however, is the result. If the campaign (now in the courts) is successful, the only marriage guidance available to the poor will be guidance that does not refer to the principal source of Jewish and Christian wisdom— and which will therefore be committed to a secular view of marriage and to the propagation of secular remedies for what are, in the majority of cases, spiritual problems. Religion will be effectively expelled from one of the areas where it is most needed, which is the repairing of damaged human relations. Moreover, those who use the Bible in counseling do so for the very good reason that it contains better advice, and a wiser understanding of human nature, than just about any other relevant text. Even if they don't believe the underlying theology, they are entitled to believe in its utility. But that may not be enough to obtain the funding needed to practice. Hence the pursuit of an abstract "freedom of religion," leads to a "freedom *from* religion." This in turn leads to a narrowing of options, with the result of promoting and privileging those that are least likely to do any good.

Still, you might say, that is not a violation of religious freedom. And that is true, in the negative sense: the withdrawal of state funding does not prevent anyone from using the Bible in counseling. It simply ensures that the Bible won't be used. On the other hand, this ideological vetting of state funds tends exactly in the direction that the "no establishment" clause was designed to prevent. And it is important to understand why. When the Constitution was drawn up the state was not in the business of taking charge of civil society, or of displacing religious and private foundations from their central role in education, health care, and the provision of social services. The "no establishment" clause did not forbid those things: it committed the state to remain neutral in the face of the existing spiritual rivalries.

Today, however, the state has intruded into civil society in a way that the Founders would never have envisaged. It does not merely fund the majority of schools: it controls them. It funds all kinds of institutions, from hospitals to rehabilitation centers, that would previously have been funded by private donations. Hence, the "no establishment" clause, interpreted as the activists would wish, obliges the state to chase religion out of the institutions of society. Having absorbed those institutions, the state fumigates them against the religious bug. But it does this *religiously,* seeking out all the nooks and crannies where religion might take hold, and squirting them with ideological disinfectant. And because the state controls the institutions where orthodoxies arise—schools and universities—it is in effect making an establishment of religion. The religion is atheism, but atheism pursued with a kind of vindictive vehemence that has all the marks of faith.

At this point it is useful to step back from the current debate, and to ask ourselves exactly what it is that religion demands of us, and just where and how the demands of religion might enter into conflict with those of the state. There are three aspects to any religion: the theological, concerning the belief in transcendental things; the ritualistic, concerning the ways of worship and the tending of sacred things; and the social, concerning general morality and the community of believers. The three aspects support one another. The belief in God, for example, renders the experience of the sacred coherent: rituals and devotional exercises put you in relation with him, and fill you with the knowledge of his love. And the community of believers is renewed through ritual, and acquires a kind of visceral unity that enables it to withstand external shock. Anthropologists and sociologists are likely to follow Durkheim in seeing religion as essentially a social phenomenon, with membership as its primary earthly goal, and theological belief as the admission ticket. For Durkheim the sacred rites gain their magic from the community that speaks through them, rather than from the transcendental beliefs which they are supposed to validate. There are religions, like the old religions of China, that remain quite vague in matters of theology, but absolutely punctilious concerning ritual. And there are religions, like some forms of Protestantism, that are the opposite, in demanding theological correctness while being largely indifferent to ritual practice. Nevertheless, for Durkheim, the social element is always vital. You *join* a religion, or are *converted* to it, and this is a matter of entering into communion with other people, and becoming a member of their church. Only in a small minority of cases does this conversion experience originate in intellectual argument or rational thought.

In allowing religious freedom, therefore, we are allowing at least three different things. We are allowing the freedom to believe certain things, the freedom to perform certain ritual observances and religious practices, and the freedom to join in communion with others. The freedom to believe is a special case of intellectual freedom. No state can control my thoughts: at best it can control their expression. The minimum requirement of religious freedom, therefore, is that I should be allowed to put my faith into words, and defend it against its detractors. This freedom certainly exists in Western countries, though it is more usual to protect it as free speech than as religious freedom.

The freedom to perform ritual observances is a freedom to *do* certain things and can be granted only if the rituals do not contravene some precept of criminal law. Some European legal systems now forbid slaughtering animals in the manner required by the ritual of 'Eid. But they are not applied, for fear of offending Muslims. Some would say that the fault lies with the law, which has intruded into matters that are not the rightful concern of the state. But this could not be said in the case of certain other aspects of Muslim observance. All of the following are practiced in the name of the faith by at least some Muslim communities in Europe: forced marriage, polygamy, female circumcision, and honor killing. All are serious crimes. Do we say, therefore, that there is no religious freedom in Europe? Surely not. To grant these freedoms, the ordinary person would argue, is to renounce the primary duty of the criminal law, which is to protect people from abuse and to reconcile the freedom of each person with the freedom of his neighbor. If there is a religion that obliges people to circumcise female children, to kill adulterous wives, or to compel girls to marry against their choice, then that religion is *itself* a threat to freedom. In saying this, however, we are covertly endorsing a principle that is recognized by Christianity but not by Islam: the principle that it is the secular jurisdiction, and not the religious law, that determines the rights and duties of the citizen. And that principle was expressly condemned by the leader of the Muslim brotherhood, Sayyid Qutb, on the authority of Ibn Taymiyya, as blasphemous.

Finally there is the freedom to join in communion with others. This is an aspect of the freedom of association that has been fought for and won in Europe and America, and which is an immovable premise of the Western way of thinking. But it has always been recognized that some associations pose a threat to the state. This is particularly so of those associations that set themselves up as a rival source of authority to the state, and which attempt to usurp its legal and political functions. Freedom of association can be granted only to associations that are genuinely *subordinate,* and that neither challenge the authority of the state in those matters that are properly the concern of political decision making, nor entertain rival legislative ambitions.

Those considerations will of course seem reasonable to people brought up in the tradition of the Judeo-Christian Enlightenment. But that tradition is a singular one that has not been replicated elsewhere in the world. The most important religious force in the modern world is undoubtedly Islam. And it is not at all clear that Islam has accepted the status of a *subordinate* association in any state where it has been able to achieve a majority. Its philosophers and political theorists have done little to delimit or to separate the spheres of politics and religion—although Ibn Khaldun made a stab at it—and it has never renounced its legislative ambitions or acknowledged that those ambitions must cede before secular authority. Does this mean that freedom of religion cannot be extended to Muslims? No, but it does mean that Muslims must renounce important traditional components of their faith, if they are to enjoy the protection of a state that guarantees their freedom. It is a general assumption of secular government in the Western tradition that those who claim a right must also confer it, and that the religious freedoms that Muslims claim in the *Dar al-harb* ought to be acknowledged and conferred in the *Dar al-islam* if our governments are to be placed under an obligation to grant them.

There is another freedom that comes into play when considering the place of Islam in the modern state, and that is the freedom to criticize. Few assaults on free speech in Western democracies have been as vehement as that now carried out in the name of Islam by its European adherents, who often regard public criticism of their faith as an intolerable offense, and may seek by threats and demonstrations to silence it. In September 2006, Rober Redeker, a French schoolteacher, published an article in *Le Figaro* arguing that Christians, when incited to violence in the name of their religion, can find no authority for this in the life and words of Christ, as recorded in the gospel, while Muslims, incited to violence in the name of *their* religion, can find plenty of support for their passions in the Koran. Although manifestly true, this statement was found to be offensive by a section of Muslim opinion, Mr. Redeker received credible death threats against himself and his family, and he and they now live in hiding under police protection. Europeans look with mounting horror and indignation on a creed that they dare not criticize, and which demands more and more space to affirm itself while yielding less and less space to its critics. It is now increasingly rare for public discussion of Islam and its stance to proceed with the open-minded concern for truth that is necessary if the discussion is to get us anywhere. Of course, mockery of another's faith is not guaranteed by freedom of speech—since mockery is a form of abuse. But it is not mockery, only, that Muslims seek to forbid: it is criticism, including the plain assertion of uncomfortable truths, such as those recently asserted by the pope in his address at Regensburg.

Freedom to criticize a religion is not a part of religious freedom; but it is one of the freedoms from which religious freedom grows. If you are allowed to criticize and even to mock Christianity, as many do, but forbidden to mock or criticize Islam, then the two faiths do not compete on equal terms. This does not mean that non-Muslims are losing their religious freedom. But the reluctance of our legislatures to take action against Islamic belligerence—to create the criminal offenses necessary to prevent the intimidation of critics and opponents—is a sign that freedom is gradually slipping down the political agenda, with appeasement taking its place, as happened before, to the great cost of Europe, with the fascists and the Nazis.

It should be clear therefore that the question of religious freedom is not only of great urgency in the world today, but also of great complexity, asking us to clarify just where freedom lies in our scheme of values. I wish to conclude this chapter, therefore, by exploring the conditions that have contributed to the freedom of religion that we have enjoyed in the West, and inquiring as to whether they could be reproduced elsewhere.

Christ, called upon to explain the law and how we must adhere to it, said this: Love the Lord thy God with all thy heart, and with all thy soul and with all thy might; and love thy neighbour as thyself. On these two commandments hang all the law and the prophets (See Matthew 22:37–40). In other words, he presented the old law of prohibitions as a *deduction* from two more fundamental commandments, which do not take the form of prohibitions but of duties, and which enjoin nothing concrete in the world of human affairs. The two duties command us to look on the world with a view to loving what we find, and must be obeyed inwardly before they can be translated into deeds. Exactly what deeds will follow cannot be demonstrated a priori, as Christ went on to show with the parable of the good Samaritan. Approaching the world in the posture commanded by Christ you are already open to legal innovation. Indeed, the law becomes just one among many instruments whereby we take charge of our lives and attempt to fill our hearts with the love of God, and our world with the love of our neighbor.

The duty to love God is further separated from the realm of civil law in the parable of the tribute money, in which Caesar's public jurisdiction is tacitly contrasted with the inner authority of religion, governing the person-to-person relationship between the individual and God: "Render therefore unto Caesar the things which are Caesar's; and unto God the things that are God's" (Matthew 22:30). Christian commentators have emphasized the duty to God, to which Christ here refers, and the need to separate religion from the taint of worldly affairs. More pertinent today is the duty to Caesar: in other words the duty to obey the civil law, and to recognize its sovereignty. Either way, Christ is making a striking pronouncement, namely, that Caesar is not God. To say such a thing, in the immediate aftermath of Augustus's claim to the contrary, is to risk being branded as a criminal. Even more striking, however, is the corollary of Christ's words, namely, that you should obey Caesar, even *though* Caesar is not a god. Taken together, Christ's words lay the foundations for a new view of law making, as a human affair, to be conducted, like everything else, in the *spirit* of religion—which is the spirit of neighbor love—but not from the *premise* of religion. Laws are no longer to be considered as God's commandments, but as the rules of coexistence. To shape them properly, we must shape them in a spirit of love; but it is we who shape them, in answer to needs of our own.

From those clear but succinct pronouncements St. Paul derived his vision of the Christian church, on the model of the Roman law *universitas*—a corporate person subject to the civil law. The Christian communities were persecuted, not because they refused to obey the law, but because they refused to worship the emperor—in other words, because they were upholding the very secular idea of jurisdiction that the Roman law had hitherto embodied, and which had been distorted by the cult of the emperor. Once Christianity had achieved legitimacy in the eyes of the civil power it went on to build the Church as an institution that is both public and subordinate: offering its jurisdiction not as an alternative to Caeser's, but as a discipline for the care of the human soul, rather than the government of civil society. Although the Church was often in conflict with the secular power, it never departed from the doctrine of the "two swords" announced by Pope Gelasius I at the end of the fifth century, according to which God has granted jurisdiction to the Church over men's souls, but to the temporal powers over the day-to-day business of the community. When the two swords are wielded by a single hand, as in the Spain of Ferdinand and Isabella, the England of Henry VIII and Thomas Cromwell, the Rome of the Farnese Papacy, or the Geneva of John Calvin, the result is a period of abnormality and upheaval, often manifest in cruel persecutions that are far from the spirit of Christian charity.

Two other historical factors played a role in the development of secular jurisdictions, both stemming from the fertile interaction of Christianity and Roman law. The first is the emergence of the *person* as a moral idea. The word *persona,* now thought to be of Etruscan origin, originally meant a mask, as worn on the theatrical stage— hence, in due course, a character in a drama. It was appropriated by the Roman law to denote the litigating subject, defined by his rights and duties, and recognized as an independent agent. The legal person was not necessarily a human being: societies, fraternities, and corporations in due course acquired legal personality. And the human individual, seen as a legal person, was an artefact, so that, as Sir Ernest Barker once put it, "it is not the natural Ego which enters a court of law. It is a right-and-duty bearing person, created by the law, which appears before the law."[1] Nevertheless, when an individual sought judgment in the Roman courts, the mask that he wore was also identical with himself. Hence, contained within the idea of the legal person were those of individual responsibility and individual right.

Defined by Boethius as "an individual substance of a rational nature," the person was later identified by Aquinas as the human essence, that in which individuality, intellect, and the moral life are all united and incarnate. Aquinas argued that the crucial part of the soul, which governs our destiny and happiness, and in which personhood resides, is the rational part, the intellect, and it is in virtue of their reason that human beings are autonomous sources of activity, spontaneously initiating events for which they are also accountable. This is what we mean, or ought to mean, by personality, and Aquinas goes on to develop a theory of the person as the highest form of creation, in which freedom, reason, accountability, and self-knowledge are given the kind of prominent position that they were later to regain, from a completely different metaphysical perspective, in Kant. The Kantian conception of freedom, that is so often represented as an Enlighten-

1. Otto Gierke, *Natural Law and the Theory of Society, 1500–1800,* trans. Sir Ernest Barker (Cambridge: Cambridge University Press, 1950), lxxi.

ment creation, is there already in St. Thomas, and foreshadowed not merely in Boethius but in the Roman law.

The other historical input deriving from the interaction of Roman law and Christianity is the idea of natural law. Roman law recognized a *ius naturalis* in addition to the *ius gentium* that applied to all subject peoples. This natural law was not a separate system of law, but a set of philosophical precepts inherited from the Stoics. Its theoretical importance, however, was far greater than its practical effect. For it gave credence to the view that there is a law contained in the nature of things, that could be discovered by human reason and which was therefore the universal property of mankind. Moreover, according to the highly influential summary of the natural law given in the seventh century by Isidore of Seville, there is a natural law of universal liberty (*omnium una libertas*), so that slavery is prohibited. This had already been recognized by the early Church, which had expanded among the slave population, and had made manumission into a religious duty. Theories of natural law were revived in the Middle Ages, following the twelfth-century *Decretum* in which someone known as Gratian (who may have been two people) summarized the Roman law inheritance and amalgamated it with biblical and ecclesiastical teachings to form the leading text of canon law. Thereafter it was generally assumed that all law either contains, or is measured against, the natural law, which is discovered by reason and implanted by God. Theories of natural law were revived in the Middle Ages, with St. Thomas once again leading the way, advocating natural law as the basis not only of moral conduct but also of the first principles of government.[2]

The effect of this was to place the free individual at the heart of politics. The individual was both the subject of government and the purpose of it. This emphasis on the individual brought to political fruition a moral and theological idea that we find in many patristic writings, not least in the *Confessions* of St. Augustine and the *De Trin-*

2. See the thorough account in John Finnis, *Aquinas, Moral, Political and Legal Philosophy* (Oxford: Oxford University Press, 1998).

itate of St. Hilary, and it could fairly be identified as the principal political legacy of the Christian faith.[3] Combined with the philosophy of the person, the theory of natural law, and the institutions of secular government, this emphasis on the individual led by its intrinsic logic to the belief in natural rights. We, all of us, on the Christian view, have rights that belong to us as human beings, that precede any particular political arrangement, and that provide a test of its legitimacy. Regimes that invade or violate the right to life, limb, and family; that enslave our bodies; or attempt to compel our faith, are regimes that transgress the boundaries of legitimate order.

The Old Testament presents us with a set of prohibitions; the New Testament with a pair of duties; the natural law with a set of rights: this progression, from prohibition, through duty, to right is contained within the dynamic of Christianity, and when reworked by Kant, so as to discard the implicit theological premise, takes on the form that is now most familiar: the form of a universal moral law, based in the sanctity of the individual. We rightly regard this as a fundamental part of our European heritage; but we seldom see that it is not an invention of the Enlightenment, but contained in a revelation granted two thousand years ago, in a Middle Eastern province of the Roman Empire.

That piece of history suggests a way in which religious freedom might be conceptualized. First, religious freedom is possible only if the claims of religion are circumscribed. To grant to a religion the freedom to extinguish religious freedom is not to grant religious freedom. A religion that makes the extinction of religious freedom into a sacred duty is not one that can be tolerated in a liberal jurisdiction, except as a minority pursuit of half-believers. Second, religious freedom is sustainable only if the spheres of religion and politics are sufficiently distinct, and the obligations of religion are sufficiently removed from the everyday aims of government. Religions that claim serious law-making powers are threats to religious freedom, unless

---

3. This has been argued from somewhat different premises by Aaron Gurevich, *The Origins of European Individualism* (Oxford: Blackwell, 1995).

those laws are confined explicitly to the private life and free association of believers, and are removed from the public sphere. Third,
while religious freedom requires the separation of state and civil society, it does not require the total disestablishment of religion, nor the
removal of all religious rites from the public institutions of a country. The important thing is not to prevent the official endorsement
of one religion, but to promote the official permission of others. The
state can make public acknowledgment of the majority faith, while
upholding the religious freedom of minorities. All that is necessary is
that the majority religion should itself permit this. Christianity manifestly both permits religious freedom and requires it. Islam, however,
neither requires it nor really permits it.

Finally, no grant of religious freedom should overlook the deep
importance of faith in the life of the believer. In granting this freedom
you are not granting a simple permission to do some trivial thing,
but the right to shape one's life, and the life of one's family according
to a complete and comprehensive plan. This right cannot be granted without permitting many things that the atheist culture finds offensive: the right to pray, to worship, to persuade; the right to acknowledge God in one's daily life, and to dedicate one's thoughts and
deeds in public gestures. Hence religious freedom, even when it can
be granted, will press up against the very limits of the space in which
our freedoms are exercised. And if it can be granted at all, it is only
because a particular religious tradition has both occupied that space,
and also relinquished it. That tradition is the Christian tradition. If we
value religious freedom, therefore, we should value the Christian faith
as its guarantee. Should the atheist culture ever triumph, so that the
voice of Christianity is silenced in our public life, this would not be a
gain in religious freedom but a loss of it. For it would leave the field
open to the two contestants that are now seeking to claim it—militant
atheism and militant Islam, both of which regard their critics as their
enemies.

two

John Finnis

RELIGION AND STATE

Some Main Issues and Sources

I

These reflections will be philosophical and historical or factual, not theological. They will draw upon and propose considerations that are available in principle to everyone and do not rely on the content of any communication that may have been made to human persons from a transcendent source by means that depart, in some measure, from the patterns that are the subjects of empirical natural and/or social sciences.

This philosophical purpose and method does not, however, have the consequence that many would assume it has, or should have. Many people assume, and some hold with argument and tenacity, that in an enquiry pursued intelligently and without bias any such transcendent source of reality and value is no more than, at most, a bare possibility. They treat as ungrounded and altogether improbable any anticipation or judgment that there has been or may well be some such communication—revelation—from such a source. But the question whether the existence and character of our universe give cogent reason for affirming the existence of such a transcendent explanation is a philosophical question, and one that cannot reasonably and philosophically be given an answer without considering, carefully and with openness, the arguments supporting such an affirmation. They are philosophical arguments, and stronger than many an argument, in many a field of philosophy, that is widely thought philosophically acceptable and warranted. I have rehearsed a number of these arguments for the existence of God in my two main books on political philosophy.[1]

Two of them are taken up by practically every serious-minded person, with degrees of clarity and resolution that differ widely from person to person and culture to culture. The first of these arguments begins by noticing how the patterns of functioning that everyone observes or infers, and that modern natural sciences successfully describe and explain, always involve a shift, change, or movement from one state of affairs (call it P) to another (call it A), such that A is the *actual* functioning of the *potentiality* so to function constituted by or present in P—a change from potentiality to act that needs explanation and is explained by some further factor, X, acting upon P and thereby bringing about the change from P to A. This line of thought proceeds

---

1. John Finnis, *Natural Law and Natural Rights* (Oxford: Oxford University Press, 1980), 378–88; *Aquinas: Moral, Political and Legal Theory* (Oxford: Oxford University Press, 1998), 298–304. In each treatment, the rest of the chapter unfolds some relevant implications, which tend to reinforce the bare initial arguments. The remarkable book by Germain Grisez that underpins especially the earlier of these two treatments has been republished with a new title and an introductory exposition of a further argument to God from practical reason's cogency: *God? Philosophical Preface to Faith* (South Bend, Ind.: St Augustine's Press, 2004).

by noticing that (as natural sciences luxuriantly illustrate) any such X is itself an actuality (call it A_1) that was shifted from potentiality (call it P_1) by another X (call it X_1) and so on. Without presupposing any denial of the possibility that the universe has existed for an infinite length of time (a possibility vigorously and repeatedly defended by Aquinas), this line of thought moves to the conclusion that the universe would be radically underexplained, and indeed could not exist, unless there is some quite different sort of explanatory factor, some sort of reality that can contribute to the explanation of every X (and thus every A and the whole universe of As) but can do so without changing or ever needing to change from potentiality to act—a sheer act(uality), free from any mere potentiality, and capable of bringing into actuality and existence anything and everything which, but for that, would and could have had no actuality at all.

Such a creative bringing of states of affairs into being also makes it possible to point to the explanation sought in the second line of thought that is pursued by any serious-minded person. This line of thought seeks to explain the orderliness of things, the orderliness and directionality of states of affairs (events and things) that (not without fortuity and disorderliness) is so thoroughly characteristic of the world we know. And the explanation sought and proposed shows that such directionality is to be understood as a direct*ed*ness resultant from something not altogether unlike our intentionally putting into effect an intelligible plan of action. This second line of thought enhances the first by showing the need to think of the transcendent pure act(uality) as intelligent and free, albeit in a manner altogether surpassing our intelligence and freedom. Thus the two lines of thought converge in the judgment that there exists a reality such as is everywhere referred to by the name "God."

The second line of thought has a further consequence. Since we have intelligence, including the capacity both to project (express) meaning and to share it, and some freedom to choose between alternatives understood by us as more or less desirable, it is reasonable to hypothesize and anticipate that there might at some time be some projection, to us, of meaning and shareable purpose, from the infinitely greater intelligence and purposiveness needed to explain the existence of our universe including our own mysterious but commonplace sharing with each other of meaning and intentions. Philosophy here bids us cast about for historical evidence of such transcendent revelation, if any there be. In doing so, philosophy does not yet consign us to theology. The judgment that certain events are best understood as instances of a transcendently revelatory communication is one that builds on the philosophically (and commonsensically) grounded affirmation of the existence of a creator, and on historically warranted affirmations that certain words were spoken and deeds done with certain intentions. The judgment draws also on the complex range of presuppositions and insights that shape judgments about personal credibility. And it also draws (or needs to be in a position to draw) on an assessment of the array of theological arguments that show that the contents of the revelation or teachings of its messengers at no point contradict reason. But none of this amounts either to making an act of faith, that is of submitting one's mind and will to the revealing God,[2] or to doing or endorsing theology, the discipline that takes as axiomatic the propositional content of divine revelation.

2. On faith and its interrelationship with the rational judgment that God exists and that a specific set of events communicates the divine purpose of creating (and, as it may be, of restoring), see Germain Grisez, *The Way of the Lord Jesus, Vol. 2: Living a Christian Life* (Quincy: Franciscan Press, 1993), chap. 1. I differ from this rich and penetrating treatment only insofar as sec. C.3 (pp. 13–14) says without qualification (such as Grisez might well wish to make) that Islam is one of the three "biblical religions" which offer a sound account of God and human persons, an account that is true humanism, forestalls modern thought's problem with free choice and objectivity, and responds to human hopes and expectations. Islam appears to me to offer unsound accounts of God, and human destiny, and to be antihumanist and unclear about free will. Above all, Islam's partial endorsement of the Bible does not at all reinforce the grounds for accepting the Bible, and where Mohammed departs from the biblical revelation and proposes an alternative account of God and salvation his teaching lacks philosophical, moral, or historical merit insofar as it differs substantially from the Bible read as it is read in the Church whose founding and teaching is witnessed to in the New Testament.

The philosophical argument to God does, however, warrant and include judgments that are theological in a broader sense. What is traditionally called "natural theology" is that part of philosophy that, while remaining strictly and integrally philosophical, speaks of such things as God's existence and nature as intelligent, free, and so forth. Similarly, despite what many say, a historical judgment of the kind hypothesized above would not cease to be authentically historical merely because it affirmed that the most reasonable explanation of certain extraordinary events is their being acts of divine revelation.

Moreover, there can be (and is) a mutual support, and in that sense interdependence, between the philosophical and the historical, each capable of giving the other a degree of clarity and certainty not available to it in isolation from the other. John Henry Newman's profound discussions of *antecedent probabilities,* from his Twelfth Oxford University Sermon (1839), through *An Essay on the Development of Christian Doctrine* (1845), to *A Grammar of Assent* (1870), bear in good measure on this network, this virtuous upward spiral, of mutually supporting considerations, presumptions, and grounds for accepting hypotheses that go, in varying ways, beyond the warrant of the simply perceptible toward—go, indeed, all the way to—responsible, critical, and warranted affirmation or confirmation not only of the transcendent and divine (affirmations of which are *primarily* philosophical) but also of concrete revelatory divine intervention, more or less preternatural, in human affairs (affirmations of which are *primarily* historical). It is such a network of convergent considerations, starting with the antecedent reasonableness of anticipating some communication between the intelligent Creator and the other intelligences in the created universe—us—that (as Newman shows)[3] subverts David Hume's a priori argument that the probability that an apparent

3. John Henry Newman, *An Essay in Aid of a Grammar of Assent,* ed. Ian Ker (Oxford: Oxford University Press, 1985), 199. I have tried to put this in the wider frame of *rationality norms;* see Finnis, *"Historical Consciousness" and Theological Foundations,* Etienne Gilson Series no. 14 (Toronto: Pontifical Institute of Mediaeval Studies, 1992), 20–21.

miracle is miraculous must always be lower than the probability that the laws of nature prevail without exception. Given the certain dependence of the laws of nature on the creative intelligence and will of an actuality not limited by any mere potentiality, it is neither contrary to nor beyond reason to expect that the course of human history might well include events, of communicative significance, going beyond or contrary to the laws that generally structure affairs. Nor need it be unreasonable to judge that such a communicative event did actually or very probably occur at such and such a time and place.

In making a responsible judgment of this kind, one will meet with another kind or instance of such rationally reinforcing interdependence: that between moral character (and the moral judgments that assess it) and the credibility of witnesses and prophets (and the factual/historical judgments that assess it). To the question whether a prophet asserting divine revelatory words or deeds is to be believed, one should indeed bring questions both about philosophical cogency and about historical evidence, but also questions about the moral creditworthiness both of the evidentiary witnesses and, perhaps even more importantly, of the supposed prophetic witness to divine communicative words or deeds of revelation. A self-styled prophet, however impressive are certain aspects of his theological teaching, undermines his credibility whenever he shows himself to be morally flawed, especially if his claim is to be the primary bearer of a new revelation and founder of new institutions or arrangements for carrying it forward in perpetuity, and especially if his moral flaws give reason to judge his supposed messages self-serving—as, for example, when he says that the God whose messenger he is has dispensed him from certain sexual restrictions, or has authorized him and his followers to require of anyone else adoption of their message on pain of death or servitude.[4] The same goes for the character and methods, morally assessed, of those who hold themselves out as witnesses to the principal prophet or founder. Apostles who are willing to kill or other-

4. See also Aquinas, *Summa contra Gentiles*, I, 6.

wise coerce, or to offer carnally seductive incentives ("the women that thy right hand possesses"), in support of their testimony and of the Prophet's message, should be contrasted with apostles who make no such threats but are willing to be killed rather than renounce their testimony or message at the demand of ruthless persons. The contrast gains in significance if it corresponds to differences in the contents of the respective revelations that these differing sets of witnesses preach. Such *moral* contrasts have great epistemic relevance. They bear directly on what is the most reasonable answer to the questions both about evidence and about substantive acceptability that are decisive for the primarily historical judgment that such-and-such is or was, or is or was not, an instance of divine revelation. And such moral contrasts also bear directly on any consequent moral decision (choice) to take the revealed message as a guide to one's actions.

II

So it was not merely a matter of taxonomy, or a mere academic concern privileging method over substance, that led me to begin these reflections on "religion and state" by pointing out the overlap between philosophy and theology, and between reason and faith. Any discussion of religion and state derails from the outset if it presumes that, as Brian Leiter puts it, "religion is contrasted with reason"[5]—a theory for which Leiter, if he felt inclined, might summon as a supporting witness the first definition of "religion" in *Webster's New Universal Unabridged Dictionary* (New York, 1992). And the discussion equally derails if it presumes that no religion's claims about God and man, world and society are reasonable, or that no religion's claims are even discussable within the domain of public reason, that is, of the discourse that one should find in universities, schools, and legislative and other political assemblies, including discourse about what laws

5. "Religious Reasons and State Power," *Brian Leiter's Law School Report,* July 26, 2006, http://leiterlawschool.typepad.com/leiter/2006/week30/index.html.

and public policies to adopt. The discussion derails, again, if it presumes that the philosophically neutral, default, baseline or otherwise presumptively appropriate framework or basis for the discussion of religion and state is that no religious claims add *anything*—whether content, certitude, or probability—to what is established in moral or political philosophy, or in natural or social science or social theory.

It derails, too, if it holds or presumes that religion's status is nothing more than one way of exercising the "right" proclaimed as fundamental and "at the heart of liberty," in *Planned Parenthood v. Casey* (1992): "to define one's own concept of existence, of meaning, of the universe, and of the mystery of human life."[6] Or again if, as Ronald Dworkin says, *the* basis of the First Amendment's guarantee of religious freedom is simply that "no one can regard himself as a free and equal member of an organized venture that claims authority to decide for him what he thinks self-respect requires him to decide for himself."[7] These celebrations of the right to "decide for oneself" and "define one's own concept" trade, as we shall see, on an important truth. But they abandon reason when they assert that the relevant intelligible and basic good in issue is not the good of aligning oneself with a transcendent intelligence and will whose activity makes possible one's own intellect and will, nor even the good of discovering the truth about some meaningful and weighty questions, but rather the good of self-determination or self-respect. For these are no true goods unless the goods around which one determines oneself deserve the respect due to what is true, rather than self-interested make-believe.

In line with one reading of some remarks of mine in *Natural Law and Natural Rights*,[8] Joseph Boyle's important paper on "The Place of

---

6. *Planned Parenthood of Southeastern Pa. v. Casey*, 505 US 833 at 851 (1992). Celebrated in the Philosophers' Brief of Ronald Dworkin, John Rawls, and others in *Washington v. Glucksberg* 521 US 702 (1997) and *Vacco v. Quill* 521 US 793 (1997): Dworkin, "Assisted Suicide: The Philosophers' Brief," *New York Review of Books* 44 (1997): 41.

7. Ronald Dworkin, *Justice in Robes* (Cambridge, Mass.: Harvard University Press, 2006), 134.

8. See *Natural Law and Natural Rights*, 90; cf. 410.

Religion in the Practical Reasoning of Individuals and Groups" (1998) argues that even "one who is not motivated by religious conviction[9] can be aware of the reason to seek—can see the point of seeking—harmony with the divine," the harmony that is Boyle's working definition, rather like Cicero's, of what *religion* is about.[10] I agree with this insofar as it points out that the line between ability and inability to recognize the good of religion does not track the line between a sound theistic belief and confused alternatives. But there are nonbelievers and nonbelievers, and radically different senses of "seeing the point" of some logically possible object of choice. One who thinks "*If* there were a divine source of reality and meaning, being in harmony with it would be a basic form of human good, but there is no *reason* to believe that there is any such source" may well, and reasonably, conclude that religion is not a basic good and indeed no good at all save as a kind—a rather imperfect, distorted and distorting kind—of self-determination, of exercise of a *Casey*-style defining of *one's own* concepts, perhaps to fit some of one's raw desires and aversions. For all who hold this sort of view of what reason—if you like, philosophy—has to say about religious claims, the place of religion in schemes of constitutional or human rights is only historically grounded. They may have no intent to set the state or its government and law against religion, still less to scorn the instrumental personal and social benefits religious belief may sometimes (perhaps often) be instrumental in yielding; but, for them, religion's constitutional status and immunities are as instances (and scarcely exemplary) of the only really basic human good, the only intrinsically worthwhile *end,* at stake: settling for oneself one's stance in the world.[11] Like Boyle, I think it is

9. Boyle has in mind here, primarily, someone who has no religious conviction and perhaps instead the conviction that all religious claims are false and there is no transcendent source of being and meaning.

10. Joseph Boyle, "The Place of Religion in the Practical Reasoning of Individuals and Groups," *American Journal of Jurisprudence* 43, no. 10 (1998): 1–24.

11. Boyle's assumption, which his article intends to test (and confirm), is "that the good of religion has rational appeal prior to such articulate beliefs about God [as that

important not to conduct one's reflections about religion and state on this false premise. The importance of not doing so is all the greater because self-determination itself is now widely regarded, not least among our constitutional lawyers, as a form, not so much of shaping up as best one can to what one judges in conscience to be reason's demands on one, but rather as the bundling of one's *strong desires,* one's "deep concerns," most considerable when most *passionate.* In such a line of thought (formalized within a year or two of *Casey*),[12] religion is doubly discredited, first by the casual assumption that it is outside the domain of reason, and then by hostility to its unwelcome critiques of and constraints upon "deep" desires. Its place in the constitution can be accepted only grudgingly as a historical relic and a monument to the threat that religions characteristically have posed to each other as well as to everyone's "conscience" (reconceptualized as the articulation of their "deep concerns").

Our reflections will go soundly if they treat affirming God as within the full reach of the critically disciplined reasoning we call philoso-

---

God is a personal being with whom cooperation is possible]"; ibid. p. 15n. That assumption may in the abstract, and in certain contexts, be sound while being unsound in a context where an understanding of the personal God of Abraham and Isaac and Jesus has been made available (not altogether inadequately) to virtually everyone. One who rejects that understanding of God is poised to reject the thesis that it is good to consider oneself in harmony, through awe and worship, with a being one has imagined or postulated. And so a good many people object to, or are puzzled by, the inclusion of religion in the list of basic goods in *Natural Law and Natural Rights.* Just as "religion presupposes some views about the divine and about the rest of reality" (p. 5), so too acceptance that religion has a distinct intelligible point presupposes the view that its views about the divine are not simply false (and demeaning).

12. Christopher L. Eisgruber and Lawrence G. Sager, "The Vulnerability of Consciences: The Constitutional Basis for Protecting Religious Conduct," *University of Chicago Law Review* 61 (1994): 1245–315 at 1266. (The title can give a mistaken impression of the authors' central thesis; they deny [pp. 1263, 1268–70] that conscience as the rational faculty of practical judgment has any more claim than religion to constitutional privilege or even protection; the proper object of constitutional protection is any "deep concern," any and all "deeply" motivated and self-shaping attitudes and behavior, which whether or not religious *or even conscientious* are all alike entitled to "equal regard".)

phy, and treat affirming the political common good (including politically acknowledged human rights) as within the full reach of critically disciplined practical reason at its highest: political philosophy. *Each* of these affirmations—of God and of a true public interest or common good—confronts openly skeptical denials, and the fair-weather friendship of fideistic or merely conventional concurrence, and the masked skepticism communicated by concepts such as Rawls's "burden of judgment" and "fact of pluralism." The "inevitably" controverted character of each of the two affirmations or affirmation-clusters only challenges us to think more resolutely, and in no way robs them of their privileged status as, in each case, the truth of the matter (or a worthwhile part of it). It is a status that *each* is entitled to, by its rational soundness.

III

Before we turn to consider how all this bears on real-life political communities, we might reflect that claims about divine revelation do not rise to the level of the philosophically considerable unless the group that advances them is willing to defend the historical assertions that are the core (albeit not the whole) of its claims. Beginning about 120 years after John Henry Newman's conversion, the Church that he joined and adored experienced a severe and still ongoing loss of faith among its members and of political and other influence in many parts of the world where it had been well established. Though the main causes of this are complex, and that Church's demanding moral teaching is prominent among them, they center, in my estimation, on the loss of confidence in the truth of those Gospel teachings that warn insistently of the utterly grave and unending consequences of one's seriously wrongful and unrepented choices. And in turn this loss of confidence derives, in some large measure, I believe, from the weakening of belief that in the four Gospels and the Acts of the Apostles we have, albeit in theologically inflected form, a truthful and sober account of things actually said and done by a man whose divine authority and, indeed, nature was attested not only by his moral authenticity and virtue but also by his transcendence to the laws of time and nature. And this weakening of belief in the historicity of the testimony of the apostles and their confidantes has among its primary causes the adoption by many of that Church's Scripture scholars, and accordingly by those whom they teach and advise, of a philosophically unsound presumption against that transcendence to laws of nature—against the miraculous.

The Gospels could be credible witnesses to everything they report even if they were written after A.D. 70. But scholars poison the root of the tree if a main reason for their concluding that a Gospel dates from after A.D. 70 is that otherwise its foretelling of the fall of Jerusalem[13] would outrun human knowledge and ignorance of the future.[14] For then the reports that Jesus foretold those events become historically discreditable, and efforts to save them from the status of falsehoods, by denying that they were intended to assert the happening or content of any actual event or statement, ripple out from these passages and change—infect—the reading of all other parts of the narrative in the Gospels (and Acts). All parts become not accounts or reports but "stories," in the equivocal terminology of the modern preacher. Of course every historical inquiry should start with a definite presumption that the events under investigation transpired in accordance with

13. Matthew 23: 37–39, 24: 1–2; Mark 13: 1–2; Luke 13: 34–35, 19: 41–44, 21: 5–6, 21–24.

14. Of course, just as scholars such as John A. T. Robinson, in *Redating the New Testament* (London: SCM Press, 1976), and John Wenham, in *Redating Matthew, Mark and Luke* (London: Hodder and Stoughton, 1991), argue from the silence of the New Testament about the circumstances and sequelae of the fall of Jerusalem in A.D. 70 to the conclusion that the Gospels and Acts antedate that event, so more conventional recent scholars may argue that features of and/or elements in the Gospels quite distinct from the *prophecies* of the fall of Jerusalem attributed to Jesus suggest a post-70 origin for Matthew and Luke if not also Mark. The point I am making does not touch the latter line of argument (though I do not find it persuasive), but concerns those who overtly or covertly assume that the prophecies are *ex eventu*—made up after the event—and employ that assumption in the approach to the dating and historicity of the Gospels.

the laws of nature. But that presumption can rationally, and should, be qualified (and in due measure, and with due caution) set aside, once a convergent set of considerations (bearing on *those* events' antecedents, concomitants, content, and sequels) make it probable that the events were part of a divine communicative intervention. For once that becomes probable, the philosophically warranted, indeed compelling, principles of methodological consistency demand that the investigation's initial presumptions, including the presumption against miracles, should be revised and indeed abandoned to the extent that the whole range of grounds for judgment makes appropriate. If Jesus of Nazareth was in any way divine, or even an authentic witness of the divine, he could speak with miraculous foreknowledge about the future of Jerusalem. So if he presumably didn't, he presumably couldn't, and so presumably wasn't divine. (The other category, "merely human messenger of the divine," is inapplicable to this man, because, if we know anything significant about what he said and did, we know that he claimed to *be* divine.) Of course, many scholars (and bishops who follow them) are inconsistent and inattentive to implications. They don't, I think, mean to run the theorem as I just did. But, like it or not, it does run that way, poison (to the proclamation of revelation) from root to leaf. A religion that remained at peace with such incoherence would drop below the horizon of philosophy, and could not claim the adherence of any earnestly enquiring mind. It would fail to live up to the demands of public reason.[15]

IV

What then does a sound philosophy of politics have to say about political communities in which there is no consensus about this

15. On public reason, coherently and critically understood, see Finnis, "Abortion, Natural Law and Public Reason," in *Natural Law and Public Reason,* ed. Robert P. George and Christopher Wolfe (Washington, D.C.: Georgetown University Press, 2000), 71–105; "Natural Law and the Ethics of Discourse," *American Journal of Jurisprudence* 43 (1999): 53–73.

world's dependence upon a divine creator, and still less consensus
about whether and if so where and how there has been any communication to us from any such creator? Even assuming (as we should)
that neither atheism nor agnosticism is the rational default position
for political philosophy, what is to be said, within political philosophy, about the place of religion in political communities, very many
of whose members treat atheism or agnosticism as their default position in both their daily lives and in their political deliberations?

These questions can be answered well by considering first a society in which adherents of sound philosophy, both political/moral and
religious, have procedurally fair and constitutional authority to settle
the laws and their execution. How should the laws and public policies
of such a state bear on religion? Answering that first form of the question will provide a sound basis for answering the question in its second form, today more engaging but inherently subordinate, about a
society that is deeply pluralist in religious beliefs, if not also about political and individual morality. My discussion focuses on the first and
basic form of the question, though some of the implications for more
deeply divided societies should become apparent.

V

Political philosophy draws on experience, including experience
which is only in a loose sense "available to all" and is better called historical. And so it is not impossible, and indeed is positively fitting, to
consider as essentially political-philosophical (and not merely positive law) that legal position on religion and state which is articulated in (1) the U.S. Constitution First Amendment's protection of "the
free exercise of religion"; in (2) the European Convention on Human
Rights article 9.1's guarantee that

> Everyone has the right to freedom of thought, conscience and reli-
> gion; this right includes freedom to change his religion or belief, and
> freedom, either alone or in community with others and in public or

private, to manifest his religion or belief, in worship, teaching, practice and observance

(subject to the considerations of public order spelled out by article 9.2); and in (3) the Second Vatican Council's Declaration (*Dignitatis Humanae*) on religious liberty. The Council's identification of the right to religious liberty closely tracks the European Convention's. Much more clearly than the Convention, however, it identifies the right not as a Hohfeldian "liberty-right" but as an *immunity*, of individuals and groups, from *coercion*—including coercion by private individuals or groups—in respect of religious belief, and all those expressions of religious belief, or other acts of putting one's religious belief into practice, that are compatible with laws motivated exclusively by concern to uphold just public order, that is (as section 7 of *Dignitatis Humanae* spells out) the rights of others, public peace, and public morality.

To show that this immunity from coercion is a natural law right, violation of which is "*intrinsically* unjust,"[16] the Council puts forward two lines of argument. The first and much more extensively expounded has as its major premise: "everyone has a moral obligation to seek the truth about religious matters, and adhere to whatever truth one finds." Then its minor premise is: "one cannot live up to that obligation in a manner appropriate to one's nature as a rational and responsible person unless one has immunity from external coercion as well as psychological freedom." The minor premise, as is usual in practical syllogisms, is essentially one of fact (albeit not brute fact)—the fact referred to by the word "cannot"—and this fact is what the Council is pointing to when in section 9 it says that "the exigencies of the dignity of the human person have become more fully known to human rea-

16. *Acta Synodalia Sacrosancti Concilii Oecumenici Vaticani II,* vol. 4 (Vatican City, 1978), 761. But should it not be admitted that this is a weak form of *intrinsece malum* (intrinsic moral wrong), since the identification of the (morally excluded) object of choice involves a reference to (further) intentions and to circumstances—namely, that the proposed coercion is not intended (or needed) for the sake of preserving the rights of others, public peace or public morality?

son through centuries of experience." This is one of the kinds of historical experience that political philosophy needs to draw upon, and can draw upon without ceasing to be philosophical.

It might be objected that coercion in religious matters does work. True, in those immediately subjected to it may induce little or nothing more than a spiritually worthless conformity to the coercing authority's demands for specified conduct or abstentions. But, so the objection goes, experience[17] shows that the children and descendants of the coerced may well live an authentic religious faith and practice in the form, or with the restrictions, coercively imposed upon their parents or forebears. To which the principal reply is that a good end, or end-state, cannot justify means which are wrong intrinsically, that is by reason of their object, that is, their proximate intention, not by reason of their further consequences. Insofar as coercion applied to P_1 has as its object a change of mind by P_1 about religious matters, it will be intrinsically wrong even if it has the consequence that P_2 and P_3 later adopt true religious beliefs by an authentic process of enquiry and reflection. That reply is not available where the object of the coercion is to stop conduct that is a violation of the rights of others or of public peace or public morality. Nor is it available where the intention in coercing P_1 is not to change P_1's religious beliefs but P_2's and P_3's. Here the reply will have to observe that the final balance sheet of consequences of those uses of coercion (just or unjust) has not yet been filled out, even from the viewpoint of the persecutors. And it will give full scope to what experience has taught about coercion's effects upon people's conceptions or misconceptions of the transcendent creator, effects alluded to by Pope Benedict XVI in his lecture on September 12, 2006, at the University of Regensburg:

17. Consider the realm of Islam, or the near extinction of England's once vibrant Catholicism over the 250 years following Queen Elizabeth's accession to the throne in 1558, or the transformation of Mormon beliefs about polygamy by remorseless use of federal coercive power between the Morrill Act of 1862 and the Mormon Church's capitulation in September 1890. The issue here is whether these repressions were effective, not whether they were justified.

The emperor [Manuel II Paleologus in his debate c. 1391 with a learned Moslem], after having expressed himself so forcefully,[18] goes on to explain in detail the reasons why spreading the faith through violence is something unreasonable. Violence is incompatible with the nature of God and the nature of the soul. "[N]ot acting reasonably ... is contrary to God's nature. Faith is born of the soul, not the body. Whoever would lead someone to faith needs the ability to speak well and to reason properly, without violence and threats.... To convince a reasonable soul, one does not need a strong arm, or weapons of any kind, or any other means of threatening a person with death."

The decisive statement in this argument against violent conversion is this: not to act in accordance with reason is contrary to God's nature.

So, as the Regensburg lecture suggests, coercion for the sake of religion has the very bad consequence of ruining people's understanding of that object (subject) of inquiry that it is most important not to misunderstand. If it be objected that the violence and unreasonableness are contrary not to the nature of God but to the human good of religion, the proper reply is that they are contrary to both. Religion as a human good is the condition of being in harmony with the transcendent providential explanatory cause of the created world, and what it is to be in that harmony cannot be rightly understood or postulated without some conception of the nature (wise? whimsically violent?) of that transcendent and personal cause. So it was with good reason that the Council began its argument for religious liberty (as an entailment of the human good of religion) with some summary reminders of the divine wisdom and love (that is, will to favor true human good, precisely for its—human persons'—objective goodness and worth).[19]

18. This alludes to a remark by the emperor, just quoted by the pope, which expresses "forcefully" an estimation of how Islam stands to biblical revelation and faith rather similar to that proposed in footnote 2 above and in the passage in Aquinas, *Summa contra Gentiles*, cited in note 4 above.

19. See Paul VI, *Dignitatis Humanae* [Declaration on Human Freedom], sec. 3.1, and note the parallel use of *suaviter* ("without force") in 1.3 and 3.1.

To support its case that coercion of religious belief, expression, and religiously motivated conduct is "intrinsically unjust," the Council adds a second, much less extensively articulated argument:

The religious acts whereby people, by their personal judgments, privately or publicly direct their lives to God transcend by their very nature the order of earthly and temporal affairs. The civil power therefore, whose proper responsibility is to attend to the *temporal* common good, ought indeed to recognize and favor the religious life of the citizenry, but must be said to exceed its limits if it presume to direct or inhibit religious acts.[20]

The repeated and key word here is "temporal," which draws in the whole tradition of thought that I summed up in my book on Aquinas's political theory like this (I abbreviate):[21]

[Aquinas judged that] God's self-communication included propositions about complete human fulfilment in eternal life; and about the community which Jesus established both to transmit that divine promise of eternal life and to help people make themselves, by free choices, ready for that life (and indeed somehow already participants in it)....

So human associations are henceforth of two fundamentally distinct types. On the one side is the "temporal" or "secular": the names connote a time-bound association and role; Aquinas uses them, in relevant contexts, as synonymous with "worldly" [mundanus] and "civil" or "political" [civilis]. The contrast is with a "spiritual" association organised, by divine inspiration, towards eternal participation (albeit in a somewhat bodily way) in the non-bodily (spiritual, mind-

---

20. Standard English translations such as that on the Vatican website are particularly poor. The text (which presents no genuine problems to translators) is: "Praeterea actus religiosi, quibus homines privatim et publice sese ad Deum ex animi sententia ordinant, natura sua terrestrem et temporalem rerum ordinem transcendunt. Potestas igitur civilis, cuius finis proprius est bonum commune temporale curare, religiosam quidem civium vitam agnoscere eique favere debet, sed limites suos excedere dicenda est, si actus religiosos dirigere vel impedire praesumat."

21. Finnis, *Aquinas: Moral, Political and Legal Theory* (Oxford: Oxford University Press, 1998), 321–22.

like) life of God.[22] The spiritual association par excellence is a church (in Latin *ecclesia*, transliterating the Greek synonym for Latin's *congregatio*); paradigmatically it is the society of "the faithful" [congregatio fidelium]....

The sole organising purpose of the Catholic Church is that there be *beatitudo perfecta* in eternal life for, so far as possible, all human persons, of every family, association, state, and people. It has no "secular" purposes. Responsibility for human affairs is thus divided between, on the one side, the Church and, on the other side, secular societies, most notably states and families....

The rationale of secular authority is, for a parent, to manage a household in which the children are nurtured and protected, fairly dealt with, and educated by instruction and discipline, in the hope that they will gain eternal life; for the law-makers and other rulers of a state, the secular mission to secure peace and justice within its territory.[23]

Aquinas himself is very clear (at the level of principle) that the coercive jurisdiction of temporal political authority extends only to external and interpersonal acts—acts that implicate the community's peace and justice.[24] Though external acts are of course, as Aquinas explains better than anyone, behavior shaped by and putting into action the internal acts that we call intending and choosing, Aquinas is firm in his assertion, if not altogether clear in his explanation, of several points. First: internal acts as such are inaccessible to human authorities;[25] main texts of his on this point were in the footnotes to *Dignitatis Humanae*'s first argument for the immunity of religious acts, in all drafts including the last.[26] Second: "personal" acts of self-disposition such as whether and

22. See *Summa Theologiae* II-II Q.183 Art. 1c; ad 2, ad 3.
23. So the "justice by which human society is governed in line with secular political good [*ad bonum civile*] can be sufficiently attained through the principles of natural right available to everyone [*principia iuris naturalis homini indita*]"; Aquinas, *de Veritate* Q. 12 Art. 3, ad 11.
24. *Aquinas,* 222–45.   25. *Aquinas,* 241.
26. Attached to the fourth sentence of para. 3 of no. 3 ("For the exercise of religion, by its very essence, consists primarily in voluntary and free internal acts by which man

whom to marry, or whether to make a religious vow,[27] are quite beyond the jurisdiction of state government and law. Third, things like "matters of faith and divine worship, and similar matters," even though everyone *ought* to do them in the same way and everyone benefits from their being done, nevertheless "do not consist in community and pertain to each individual person in himself [*ad unum aliquem pertinet secundum seipsum*]."[28] Aquinas's philosophical arguments for these positions are the arguments deployed in *Dignitatis Humanae*—arguments from the essential interiority and inaccessibility of such acts, and from the limitation of the state's coercive jurisdiction to matters that are public, not purely private—though Aquinas supplements his arguments by appeal to the essential equality of persons, and *Dignitatis Humanae* raises the whole set of arguments to a new plane by making primary one's serious duty to pursue the truth about ultimates and to shape one's life in line with what one judges one has discovered about them, a duty that is only fulfilled if it is pursued with an authenticity that coercion and "psychological pressure" prejudice, corrupt and tend to nullify.

Adding clarity and certitude to the philosophical arguments both of Aquinas and the Council are the Declaration's theses of (as it asserts) divine revelation and divinely guided ecclesiastical tradition: the division of jurisdiction implicit in "Render to Caesar the things that are Caesar's, and to God the things that are God's," and from the earliest apostolic times onward the unbroken refusal to countenance any attempt to coerce someone to embrace the Christian faith against his or her own will.[29] Indeed, all the elements of the Council's declaration of a natural, human right to religious liberty are taken from

directly orders himself to God: acts of this kind cannot be commanded or prohibited by merely human authority") was the footnote: "Cf. S. Thomas, ST I-II Q. 91 Art. 4c: 'Man can make laws about those matters about which he can judge. But there can be no judgment of man about interior acts which are hidden, but only about exterior acts which are manifest'; cf. II-II Q. 104 Art. 5c: 'In matters which pertain to the interior movement of the will, man is not bound to obey man but only God.'"

27. *Aquinas*, 239–41.
28. *Summa contra Gentiles* III c. 80 nn. 14, 15; *Aquinas*, 226. 253–24.
29. Paul VI, *Dignitatis Humanae*, sec. 10.

authorities as traditional as Aquinas, and none of the *principles* defended by Aquinas is contradicted. As the drafting committee advised
the Council fathers orally and in writing in the two days before the
final vote adopting *Dignitatis Humanae,* the old thought that error
has no rights remains unchallenged. Understanding "liberty" in its
strict (Hohfeldian) sense—absence of duty—there is no moral liberty
to proclaim a false religion.[30] But there is the human right (Hohfeldian claim-right) to be immune from coercion by individuals, groups,
governments, or laws, in one's religious or religiously motivated acts,
provided they are in line with public order; and the acts thus immune
include adhering to and proclaiming a religion that one believes to be
true but is in fact false. Taking common good in its widest extension,
it is for the common good of the members of a political community
that they find the truth about divine creation and redemption, live in
accordance with that truth, and so enter and remain forever in the
altogether fulfilling fellowship of the divine family extending from
this world into eternity. But the state is responsible only for temporal common good, and correspondingly the coercive jurisdiction of
state government and law has as its defining objective not the widest
common good that might include salvation itself, but what the Council calls a (or the) "basic component of the common good," namely
public order.[31] The entire shift away from medieval and early modern, ecclesiastically sponsored practices of state coercion of, or arising
out of, religious beliefs and acts is carried out by a shifted emphasis
among, a clarifying reordering of, a set of truly perennial principles.

VI

Philosophically assessed, without the philosophically unsound
presupposition of atheism or agnosticism about creation and reve-

---

30. *Acta Synodalia Sacrosancti Concilii Oecumenici Vaticani II,* vol. 4 (Vatican
City, 1978), 720–22, 725 (response to "general *modus*" no. 2, repeated by cross-reference
twenty times in subsequent responses to *modi*).

31. Paul VI, *Dignitatis Humanae,* sec. 7.

lation, the natural law thesis articulated in *Dignitatis Humanae*, like its positive law antecedents in the U.S. Constitution and the European Convention on Human Rights, constitutes a sound and true civilizational core. It is a centering pole between unsound secularist and theocratic alternatives.

Secularists, presuming or asserting that religion cannot be grounded in rational enquiry that issues in true judgments, may nonetheless remain within the tradition of their society and admit religious concerns and acts among the "grand diversity of relationships, affiliations, activities, and passions that share a constitutional presumption of legitimacy" because in them (as Eisgruber and Sager put it) the members of "a modern, pluralistic society ... find their identities, shape their values, and live the most valuable moments of their lives."[32] Religious acts, they concede, have the same dignity and constitutional status as the "relationships, affiliations, activities and passions" under discussion. Eisgruber and Sager's article does not say how far this wider category extends, but it seems they would include (and not merely marginally) the activities in issue in in *Bowers v. Hardwick*[33] and *Lawrence v. Texas*,[34] and likewise those in *Roe v. Wade*[35] and *Planned Parenthood v. Casey*,[36] activities which often, it is not unreasonable to suppose, express not so much conscience or any other concern for truth as very strong (deep) emotional desires of the kind that are so often the subject of belated rational regret.[37] Secularists differently placed

32. Eisgruber and Sager, "The Vulnerability of Consciences," 1266.

33. *Bowers v. Hardwick*, 478 US 186 (1986).

34. *Lawrence v. Texas*, 539 US 558 (2003).

35. *Roe v. Wade*, 410 US 113 (1973) .

36. *Planned Parenthood of Southeastern Pa. v. Casey*, 505 US 833 (1992).

37. True, sometimes acts of the kinds in question (acts of nonmarital intimacy, elective abortions) are sought for conscience sake, and religious acts are sometimes or even rather often performed for reasons other than conscience. But Eisgruber and Sager's argument looks only to the "deepness" (and in that equivocal sense authenticity) of the concern that underlies the protected class of activities, and sets aside any requirement (whether at the level of explanatory principle or of constitutional test) that the concern and self-determination have the *responsibility* (ultimately to truth and

have often drawn conclusions less favorable to constitutional respect for or even tolerance of religion, as we have seen in many places over many decades of the twentieth century.

And at the other end of the spectrum at whose center stands *Dignitatis Humanae* are the theocracies. These are exemplified in the early modern world by Elizabethan and Jacobean England—in which citizens are directed to perform the religious acts of a worshipping community that is treated as coterminous with the state and whose leaders and ceremonies are specified directly by the state's government. Today they are exemplified by the two main Islamic forms, Sunni, in which like Anglican England the state appoints religious leaders, and Shi'ite, in which (like Puritan England and Calvinist Geneva) the political community and all its members are subject to the coercive control and jurisdiction of the religion's leaders. Radicalized, in ways that have not convincingly been shown to be unfaithful to the core texts or traditions of Islam's purported divine communication, these two forms can together be called Islamism, which in its outward-looking aspect often describes itself as Jihadism, and has a variety of forms that it is not necessary here to itemize.

It is worth adding one further factual observation about the present disposition or alignment of civilizational blocs, groupings, or "forces." Just as the Catholic Church's doctrine of religious liberty is pointedly aimed, in one direction against secularist (say American) devaluation of the earnest search for truth about religion and life and secularist (say Communist) repression of religion, and in the other direction against antiphilosophical and anti-Christian (not to mention anti-Semitic) theocratism, so too that Church's members, in their political and day-to-day involvement with issues very fundamental to the legal protection of life and freedom, find themselves allied, variously, with each of those ends of the spectrum against the other. That is part of what it is to be central to civilization.

_____

thereby also to other persons) and alertness to intrinsic *worth* implicit in conscience and religion.

VII

So state governments and legal systems have a negative duty: not to coerce religious acts unless these threaten the rights of others, public peace, or public morality. Have they other negative duties, perhaps the duty not to discriminate between adherents of one religion and adherents of another? And have they any positive duties, say (as we have seen *Dignitatis Humanae* saying) to encourage the religious activities of citizens, or again to perform what the Council calls[38] "the moral duty of men and societies toward the true religion and toward the one Church of Christ"?

Joseph Boyle gives the following positive formulation to the negative duty, and to the Council's arguments for it from authenticity and jurisdiction. His formulation is one that seems to enhance the duty's negative implications by cutting off any favor for a particular religion, any disfavor for a specific religion, and any favor for religion over irreligion or for irreligion over religion:

> Political society is morally obliged to create the social space for people to fulfil their obligation to seek the truth in religious matters and live accordingly. *It cannot do this if political life is conducted as if a certain outcome of this inquiry—whether a particular kind of belief or nonbelief—were correct*; for such political action skews public life in ways that hinder rather than facilitate this inquiry, and inevitably and unfairly *coerces* some to support actions whose rationales are incompatible with deep elements of their worldviews. Rather, political society must recognize that its proper actions cannot be based on any particular outcome of this morally mandatory inquiry, since the correctness of any such outcome is for individuals, families, and voluntary associations, not political societies, to determine.[39]

Boyle here uses the notion of coercion a good deal more expansively than *Dignitatis Humanae*, since he includes governmental ac-

---

38. Paul VI, *Dignitatis Humanae*, sec. 1.

39. Boyle, "The Place of Religion in the Practical Reasoning of Individuals and Groups," 22 (emphases added).

tions whose intentions are not to coerce anyone but to favor some, so that any coercive effect is a side-effect. But, as a matter of political philosophy or natural law or human rights, may it not be true that (as Boyle seems to be saying) the immunity of religious acts from coercion extends to policies, especially governmental policies that, albeit as a side-effect, have a coercive impact on those who do or might do religious acts? And may it not also be true that the state's favor for one religion over others, or over irreligion, might entail that the state was making religious judgments, something outside its proper sphere and responsibility? As the prospectus for these lectures puts it, seeming to take a view like Boyle's: "the principled respect for the autonomy of the individual person expresses itself in the form of principled neutrality on the competing claims of diverse religious communities."

A reflection in response to Boyle and to the lecture prospectus might begin with the Equality Act 2006, s. 52(4)(g), which exempts from that United Kingdom statute's prohibition of discrimination on grounds of religious belief (or unbelief) the following class of decisions by public authorities:

> (g) a decision in connection with an application for entry clearance or for leave to enter or remain in the United Kingdom or anything done for the purposes of or in pursuance of a decision of that kind ... if the decision is taken on the grounds—
> (i) that a person holds an office or position in connection with a religion or belief or provides services in connection with a religion or belief, [or]
> (ii) that a religion or belief is not to be treated in the same way as certain other religions or beliefs, or
> (iii) that the exclusion from the United Kingdom of a person to whom paragraph (i) applies is conducive to the public good.

Though this authorization of discrimination between religions in immigration decisions is narrow, not to say timid, if it is to be understood as covering only a religion's functionaries, rather than any or all of its other nonnational members, the provision nonetheless gives us one way of testing Boyle's thesis.

Suppose a general decision is taken by the British authorities that the functionaries of a certain religion are to be excluded on the ground that that religion "is not to be treated"—regarded, assessed, and acted upon—in the same way as most or all other religions precisely *because* its functionaries teach, or incline its adherents to believe (say), (i) that any who speak adversely of its prophet or decline specific invitations to convert may appropriately be intimidated, assaulted, or killed, or (ii) that the British state and its institutions should be subordinated to this religion's laws authorizing coercion of religious acts, polygamy, and other violations of British constitutional law and what the British authorities regard as natural law and human rights. Such a general decision, even though restricted to the immigration or expulsion of such functionaries, would be a governmental decision precisely about the content of a religion (at least in the form in which it is ascertainably held by those functionaries and their followers). It would reasonably be taken by everyone to presuppose the judgment that the religion (as so held and professed) is false at least *pro tanto*. It would in both those ways skew public life against that religion, and would begin to put pressure on its adherents or potential adherents, pressure of a kind that Boyle's line of argument seems to treat as coercion by side-effect if not by intent. Yet it might well, I suggest, be an entirely reasonable decision properly and perhaps urgently required by what the act calls "the public good" and what *Dignitatis Humanae* and the European Convention call public order, notably the rights of others and public peace.

For it is a very grave degradation of public order and the temporal common good that there has recently been imported into our polities religious intimidation, extending perceptibly into the operations of the media, the academy, the writing of lectures such as this, and many other institutions of national life. The exclusion or expulsion of those nonnationals who give open or covert or tacit support to the religious doctrines and practices of intimidation is in principle compatible, I suggest, with the true right to religious liberty.

So I do not think that England's highest court must be said to have erred in the recent Shabina Begum case when, interpreting the *European Convention on Human Rights,* it dismissed the claim that a state school violated religious liberty when it banned its pupils from attending school clad not in any of the school's prescribed choice of Western- or Muslim-style alternative school uniforms but in a more austere garment of the kind demanded by more militant forms of Islam. The law lords used as the decisive premise in most of their judgments the factual and legal findings of the Constitutional Court of Turkey, adopted also by the European Court of Human Rights,[40] that (1) where Islam (as distinct from other religions) is socially influential even the *option* of wearing to school or university a distinctively Muslim form of attire is regularly and predictably the occasion and opportunity for intimidatory pressures, and (2) state governments and laws and other public institutions are accordingly entitled to exclude and forbid that sartorial exercise of religious liberty, in order to preserve public order including the religious liberty of others (and even, sometimes—perhaps often—of the would-be wearer herself).[41] The lords' decision implicitly accepts the premise that one religion may and should be treated—understood and dealt with—differently from others (just insofar as its beliefs and practices, perhaps even core beliefs and practices, adversely affect public order, public morality, or the rights of others).[42] And the lords' decision should remind us that the right to be free from coercion in one's religious beliefs and acts is a right that is good not only against the state and its government and

40. *Şahin v. Turkey,* 41 EHRR 109 (2004); see *R (Begum) v. Headteacher and Governors of Denbigh High School*—UKHL 15 at 32 (Lord Bingham), 59–65 (Lord Hoffmann), 91 (Lord Scott), and 98 (Baroness Hale) (2004).

41. *R (Begum) v. Headteacher and Governors of Denbigh High School,* UKHL 15 (2006).

42. Only if and to the extent that it is compatible with this rightful discrimination between religions should one accept the assertion of Jürgen Habermas, *Between Naturalism and Religion* (Cambridge: Polity Press, 2006), 151–81; that "The principle of separation of church and state demands that the institutions of the state operate with strict impartiality vis-à-vis religious communities."

laws, but also against all other individuals and social groups. If a religion treats coercion of its own adherents, or potential adherents, or of anyone else as permissible, let alone mandatory, it is a standing incitement to violate the rights of others and public order, and those who adhere to it faithfully are rightly liable, in principle, to be kept or, where morally possible, as far as is necessary from political communities that acknowledge the right to religious freedom.

VIII

Joseph Boyle might respond, however, that I have mistaken the focus and exaggerated the reach of his concern that unintended social pressure may impact as coercion impacts on the authenticity and worth of religious behavior chosen under such pressure. His concern, he might respond, was not with governmental attempts to defend public order from real religious threats. Even though such legitimate defenses of public order may presuppose the falsity of a part of the creed of a particular religion, they need not intend to teach or proclaim that falsity, or anything about the truth or otherwise of that religion or any other religion. Boyle's concern, he might say, was rather with constitutional or governmental declarations intended to identify the correct answer to the question whether there is a true religion. Such declarations cannot plausibly claim to be made for the sake of public order, and (Boyle might say) not only overreach the due limits of the jurisdiction of state government and law, but also create a social pressure prejudicial to the authenticity of religious inquiry and faith. So, he might conclude (and does already, I think, imply), there can be no positive duty of state government and law toward the true religion as true (but only the general negative duty owed to all religious communities respectful of the just limits of public order, the duty not to coerce their religious beliefs or practices).[43]

43. Here as earlier I leave aside the issue much debated in U.S. constitutional doctrine whether religious acts are presumptively immune ("exempt") from the operation

Inquiring whether a state's law and government can justly adopt a religion as true does not seem of urgent practical importance. But, urgency aside, it will clarify our political-theoretical reflections to keep that question before us, like a distant peak, and approach it via the foothills.

First, then, the main strands of my reflections entail that the state's government and law cannot justly teach that no religion is true. For such a teaching would be false, and false on a matter closely affecting a basic aspect of human well-being. And if a state does not teach that but its arrangements give rise, as a side effect, to widespread belief that the state's government has adopted them because it holds that no religion is true, the government has a significant duty to do what it reasonably can to rebut that inference. This it can do most readily by following, in ways that are for it to determine, the Vatican Council's injunction to "recognize and favour religion." It is hard to see how government might otherwise counteract the damaging side effect and false inference than by measures that carry a countervailing implicit message that some religion may well be essentially true and that if so the others, for all their errors, at least have the benefit of mediating the important truth that there is a transcendent source of being, intelligibility, and value.

The U.S. Constitution's prohibition of "establishment of religion," as that is interpreted, gives rise to problems hereabouts, which I need not dwell upon. British and other European constitutional arrangements that contain no such provision confront a different problem hereabouts. They can favor religion to the extent needed in justice—namely, by implying if not asserting that some religion may well be true—and can do so by requiring or permitting the teaching and profession of religious faith in state-run or state-funded schools (with suitable opt-outs to preserve religious liberty). But the threat that

---

of legal commands or prohibitions of general applicability to religious and nonreligious acts alike (i.e., "neutral" as between religiously motivated acts and acts not so motivated).

some religious beliefs present to public order (essentially by authorizing or inciting intimidation), and present in the longer term to the constitutional order that enforces the right to religious liberty, may be such that it is necessary to explicitly withhold from those beliefs the advantages that parity with other religions, combined with weight of numbers, would otherwise require. Such discrimination, though justified, runs so strongly against widespread assumptions about "equal protection of the laws" that governments will be sorely tempted to withdraw their favor from all religions, rather than make "invidious comparisons and choices." Yielding to the temptation would create, even if only as a side effect, the very bad consequence of seeming to express the belief that no religion is true. To incur that consequence deliberately is presumptively unjust. So the discrimination should presumptively be made, with all due care for accuracy and procedural fairness.

Secondly, however we should answer the peak question (about what if anything may be stipulated constitutionally and legally about the true religion), there is certainly an obligation not to hold out as true any religion that is not essentially the true one.

Thirdly, there is a duty not to make subscription to a particular religion, or to one of the many religions, a prerequisite for public offices or benefits. For, subject perhaps to some minor exceptions, such an affirmative "religious test" does have coercive effects of the kind that Joseph Boyle points to as tending to negative authenticity, and does exceed the state's proper bounds. Only when the upholding of public order requires it can it be right to accept those bad side effects of imposing a negative test such that membership in a religious group threatening to public order becomes a *dis*qualification for public office.

Fourthly, there is a duty not to seek to *direct* the true religion by claiming a power to appoint its functionaries (say, bishops) or to give or withhold ratification of its doctrinal pronouncements or ecclesiastical arrangements.

Fifthly, however we should answer the peak question, it must be accepted that individual voters and legislators can rightly and should take into account the firm moral teachings of a religion if it is the true religion, so far as its teachings are relevant to issues of law and government. This duty extends only so far as the teachings do not depend upon premises that are essentially questions of present fact and prediction of consequences, for on such questions religious authorities cannot reasonably be supposed to have any special competence, or authority to teach with any decisive effect. In saying that voters and other bearers of public authority have this liberty and responsibility, I assume that the true religion itself holds out its moral teaching as a matter of public reason, that is, as accessible and acceptable by a purely philosophical enquiry and only *clarified* and/or made *more* certain by divine revelation or the theological-doctrinal appropriation of that revelation. And I assume that this holding out is no mere lip service or idle boast, but goes along with real willingness to shoulder the argumentative burden of making its moral and political teaching philosophically plausible, and maintaining the educational and scholarly resources for doing so.

Sixthly, then, I think we can give at least this response to the peak question: with the third duty firmly acknowledged as excluding *positive* religious tests for voting or other public office, and with the negative duties to abstain from coercion all firmly in place, it does not seem to be contrary either to what experience shows are the exigencies of authenticity in religious enquiry, or to what seem likely to be the conclusions of revelation as well as philosophy about limits to the state's coercive jurisdiction and temporal authority, to hold that in establishing their constitutional arrangements a people might without injustice or political impropriety record their solemnly held belief about the identity and name of the true religious faith and community.

Even when politically possible, making such a declaration might in many circumstances have such bad side effects that doing so would be unfair or otherwise unreasonable. And it would always be a quite unfitting declaration to make if the adherents of the religion so identified did not accept and act on the responsibility that I mentioned earlier, of showing how their faith embraces and is continuous with public philosophical, historical, and moral reason.

three

Livio Melina

THE ECLIPSE OF THE SENSE OF

GOD AND MAN

"The Lord God called to the man, and said to him: 'Where are you?'" (Gen. 3:9). Ever since man withdrew from his dialogue with God he appears to have been swallowed up and to have disappeared into the world of nature, or even worse, become confused with the world of objects. And he is not even able to find himself. The voice that seeks him from the depths of his conscience is drowned in the deafening din of the sounds made by his doings and the clamor of his dazzling successes. It causes disquiet, but does not manage to provoke a return home from that land of dissimilarity (*regio dissimilitudinis*), where he is wandering.[1] How long has he been hiding? Why has he been hiding? But, above all: Where is he hiding?

1. In this regard, please consult the inspiring meditation of S. Grygiel, "*Errantes revoca:* Essai sur l'auto conscience, sur le péché et la réconciliation," *Anthropos* [now

Biotechnology and the "Posthuman" World

It seems right to look for him starting with the crucial question that scientific progress itself puts to him with a new radicality. The era of biotechnology has begun, placing in man's hands a growing power not only to acquire better health, but to change his own natural faculties. It now allows him to go "beyond therapy," manipulating even his corporal genetic structure so as to fulfill his desire for "better children, superior prowess, younger more beautiful bodies, sharper minds and happier dispositions."[2] In its pursuit of happiness, biotechnology considers human corporality mere raw material, to be shaped at will.

But reducing man to raw material for unusual experiments on himself[3] places him before the worrying question of who will lead such a process, that is who, in the end, will conduct the game. Who is doing the experimenting and what is being experimented upon? Impersonal experimentation is done on "things" that can be manipulated: both the subject and object of experimentation are lost in the imposition of a law that appears to overtake both with its implacable need. To paraphrase C. S. Lewis, we should ask ourselves whether what at first sight appears to be man's dominion over nature does not paradoxically become completely the reverse in the absence of a knowledgeable hand to guide the action and become nature's dominion over man himself.[4] By hiding God from man, scientific progress has hidden man from himself and runs the risk of completely losing sight of him, going past him as if he were a transitory moment in a

---

Anthropotes] (1985): 13–29. There is also the classic study by E. Gilson, *"Regio dissimilitudinis de Platon à St Bernard de Clairvaux,"* *Medieval Studies* 9 (1947): 108–30.

2. L. Kass, *Beyond Therapy: Biotechnology and the Pursuit of Happiness: A Report by the President's Council on Bioethics* (New York: Regan Books–HarperCollins, 2003), 274–310.

3. M. Jongen, "Der Mensch ist sein eigenes Experiment," *Die Zeit,* August 9, 2001, p. 31.

4. C. S. Lewis, *The Abolition of Man* (New York : Macmillan, 1965), 72–80.

necessary process of nature that evolves blindly, with no human aims to pursue any more.

Faced with the prospect of a "posthuman world" that could end by turning against man himself, the only defense, in the eyes of many people, would appear to be a return to a definition of natural rights based on human dignity.[5] Yet this is precisely where the aporia of the situation in which we find ourselves is laid wide open. The subject of human rights always involves some anthropology and some conception of human nature.[6] To propose a definition of this nature based on human sciences, genetics, or the environment, does not guarantee a point of reference capable of guiding biotechnology at all. Moreover, any kind of knowledge that differs from the purely scientific, or pragmatic and calculating, is banned from public circles. Thus, the question of a knowledge of human nature able to inform man's increasingly powerful interventions on himself, would appear to be both *imperative* and *impossible,* at least from a scientific point of view. It is also extremely *urgent,* being not only a matter of theory but also and necessarily of practice in life and the unavoidable choices that life entails at the social as well as the personal level.

The harm inherent in the activities of modern science and the civilization built upon it was perceived and described by the fathers of Vatican Council II who, in the document *Gaudium et Spes,* after having recognized the legitimate autonomy of earthly affairs, warned however that we should not think about them without referring to the Creator, for "without the Creator the creature would disappear, ... indeed to forget God is to deprive that same creature of light" (n. 36).[7] Along the same lines and with even greater alarm, John Paul II contin-

5. With regard to this issue, see F. Fukuyama, *Our Posthuman Future: Consequences of the Biotechnology Revolution* (New York: Farrar, Straus and Giroux, 2002), 237.

6. A. M. Rouco Varela, *Los fundamentos de los derechos humanos: Una cuestión urgente,* ed. Fernando Gonzalez (Madrid: Real Academia de Ciencias Morales y Politicas, 2001).

7. H. De Lubac's reflections on the subject, "*Le drame de l'humanisme athée*" (Paris: Spes, 1945), was prophetic and quite likely inspired the conciliar fathers.

ued with the reflection in the encyclical *Evangelium Vitae,* stating that "when the sense of God is lacking, the sense of man is also threatened and poisoned," because he ends by not recognizing that he is unique among the other living creatures, and, locked in his narrow physical confines, is reduced to "a thing" completely open to domination and manipulation (n. 22).

If at the heart of man's eclipse from himself lies the eclipse of God the Creator from the boundaries of modern civilization, our reflection is prompted to explore the two areas of reasoning from which any reference to God has been purposely excluded: science and public morality, to seek the motives of such a delimitation and the why of its possibly permanent reasonableness in the light of the above mentioned aporia.

Scientific Rationality and Religious Belief

In the dawn of modern science, one of its most emblematic figures, Galileo Galilei, proposed a thesis, designed to avoid conflict between the new Copernican astronomy and the Holy Scriptures. They dealt with two entirely different subjects: the former had to do with factual matters, the latter with the salvation of men. In a letter to Christine de Lorraine in 1615 he wrote: "I would here like to say what I understood from a very high ranking ecclesiastical personage, and that is that the intent of the Holy Spirit is to teach us how we may go to heaven and not how the heavens go."[8] It is the thesis of the great divide between the scientific and religious spheres, by means of which Galileo, who was not only an eminent scientist but also a profoundly religious man, thought to avert conflict. The spheres of competence are indeed separate and autonomous, referring to different methods, criteria, and sources. Although on other occasions he had preferred to speak of the harmony and convergence between the book of nature, investigated by the sciences, and that of the Holy Scripture, in

8. M. Pera, "Introduzione: Una proposta da accettare," in J. Ratzinger, *L'Europa de Benedetto nella crisi delle culture* (Siena: Cantagalli, 2005), 8–9.

the end he believed that the only compelling conclusions with respect to worldly matters were the scientific ones.[9]

The stand of the great Florentine scientist is easily understood, in its concern to defend the autonomy of scientific reasoning from any undue intrusion on the part of faith. Science had to be free to proceed on its own account, even if the Scriptures were to be against some particular point or another. At its core lies the implicit conviction that the only authentic knowledge is scientific knowledge, whereas in the case of faith, it is rather a matter of belief than knowledge. The unity of knowledge is thus split between public and objective knowledge, and subjective and private belief.

However, the latent conflict erupts when the close link between modern science and technology is considered. The knowledge of the former is in effect at the service of the power of the latter, which is bent on intervening in the world in order to change it, and is consequently also obliged to claim its freedom from religion as well. The novelty of modern science is that it no longer understands itself to be a cognitive event and an end in itself, but that it inserts itself in the history of man to act as a guide and direct the task of transforming and humanizing man and the world.

However, as Martin Heidegger perspicaciously pointed out, technological thinking, which is so robust and efficient in discovering means, is not neutral at all, but implies a very clear view of reality and a correlated concept of human freedom.[10] The technical or instrumental dimension of reason that produces efficient means has overcome the philosophical or sapiential one that seeks to discover ends. Not only religious belief, but every type of knowledge different from scientific knowledge is marginalized and banished from what is considered verifiable and universally accepted. The condition for this unilateral type of reasoning to prevail is the negation of the idea that there exists a truth of creation that has to be respected. If that is

9. Galileo's letter to Benedict Castelli dated December 21, 1631, in ibid, 7.

10. M. Heidegger, *Vortrage und Aufsatze* (Neske: Pfullingen, 1954), 29–31.

the case, then everything can be manipulated without limit except-
ing the calculation of one's own advantage. If the coming into being of
the world does not depend upon a creative act of God, if it is not an
expression of his sagacious design, whose ends have to be discovered
and respected, but a matter of chance, then everything can be different from what it is and everything can be manipulated at will.

The main ethical challenge of our times, as Hans Jonas said, is
composed of two converging factors: the metaphysical degradation of
man due to modern science and the enormous growth of his power
due to technology.[11] Technical knowledge of human life has not only
predominated over wisdom and refused to be guided by it, but is also
presuming totally to replace any residual sense of mystery, reducing
life's decisive and delicate moments to a technical act.

Should reality be deprived of an intrinsic meaning given it by the
Creator, then it is reduced to a material that can be manipulated by
the creative conscience of man. In that case practical rationality loses
any possible reference to a preceding content, and in turn it too becomes a creator of meaning.

As a result of this observation it becomes necessary to submit to
criticism the method implicit in sciences, which is in substance "ana-
lytic" in that it literally proceeds via the breaking of the bonds that
unite things, thereby reducing that which is whole and unitary into
easily controlled and dominated parts, like the various parts of a ma-
chine, a simple "*res extensa*," to be split up. Any possible affirmation
of God in this system, as David L. Schindler observes, can come at the
most from an extrinsic basis, with no direct influence on the mechan-
ical development of the events that concern the world.[12] The God
who might possibly be acknowledged is a clockmaker God, author of
the mechanism that once it starts to work is self-sufficient, a God who
could easily be dead.

11. H. Jonas, *Dalla fede antica all'uomo tecnologico* (Bologna: Il Mulino, 1991), 262.
12. D. L. Schindler, *Heart of the World, Center of the Church: Communio Ecclesiol-
ogy, Liberalism, and Liberation* (Grand Rapids, Mich.: Erdmans, 1996), 189–202.

To limit reason to that which can be tested or calculated is not only replete with negative consequences on a practical level, but it is also intrinsically contradictory. The rationality of the universe cannot be explained reasonably on the basis of an ultimate irrationality. The fact of reflecting on the development of sciences implies a synergy between the mathematical hypotheses formulated and their verification through testing, which sends us back to an original Logos, as a condition to make such correspondence possible. In this manner even what modern science undertakes brings us back to the idea of a creator Logos, as being "the best hypothesis" and therefore to the Christian context as the humus where it was born and able to develop.[13] Thus we have reached a first result: even scientific rationality needs to recognize a broader and more founding rationality, open to the mystery of a creator Logos, in order to preserve itself. Moreover, its method and applications need to be kept under continuous critical control, but this can come only from a more synthetic knowledge of reality, in harmony with this original Logos.

The "Impious" Hypothesis of Huig de Groot

Let us now turn to the other dimension of rationality, from which modernity has purposely excluded any reference to God: public morality. Here we find a typically European experiment, worked out halfway through the seventeenth century in "the land where the sun sets," but which casts its shadow over the whole of the West and is doing so today at the global level. I refer to a proposal put forward by the Dutch lawyer and theologian Huig de Groot, known as Hugo Grotius, in his treatise *De Iure Belli ac Pacis,* to found natural law, which is the foundation of social life, "*etiamsi daremus, quod sine summo scelere dari nequit, non esse Deum aut non curari ab eo negotia humana.*"[14]

13. J. Ratzinger, *L'Europa di Benedetto,* sec. 103–24.

14. H. Grotius, *De Iure Belli ac Pacis,* Prolegomena §11 (1646). Notwithstanding the fact that the origin of the Grotian doctrine is uncertain, analogous expressions are to be

Social life has to be based on rules that flow from rights established by autonomous reason and that are valid even on the assumption, which even Grotius himself defines as "impious," that God does not exist or that he is not concerned with the affairs of men. It was just a hypothesis, it was not affirmed, on the contrary, it was explicitly rejected by the author, but it was significant because it proposed a methodological exclusion of religion from the foundations of public life of society.

As Wolfhart Pannenberg pointed out, such a proposal had to be understood in the context of the denominational divisions and religious wars that afflicted Europe between the second half of the sixteenth century and the first half of the following one.[15] Confronted with the shattering of the Christian universe and the evident impossibility of founding social coexistence on a common religious basis, the humanists of modern times turned to reason as the only source able to provide universal moral certainties that could be shared by all of society. Religion appeared to be the source of division and war, while only a rationality that kept its distance from religion could guarantee peace and coexistence among peoples.

However, this started the process of secularization that tended to exclude God completely from the public conscience, relegating him to the private sphere. "God, if there is one, has nothing to do with it," was the formula coined by Cornelius Fabro to describe the basic principle of this mentality, not necessarily atheistic, but at least deistic if not agnostic.[16] God has nothing to do with the everyday life of men, with the social choices they make or their interests and affairs. Expelled from the fervor of life on earth and the shaping of the communities of men, God loses interest, becomes useless, could even be

---

found in Occamists like Gregorio da Rimini (1290–c. 1380) and Gabriel Biel (1410–95), and also in Gabriel Vasquez (1551–1604).

15. Wolfhart Pannenberg, *Ethik und Ekklesiologie. Gesammelte Aufsätze* (Gottingen: Vandenhoeck & Ruprecht, 1977), 55–69.

16. Luigi Giussani, *Il senso di Dio e l'uomo moderno* (Milan: RCS Libri SpA, 1994), 95–99, quotes this expression from Cornelio Fabro, *Introduzione all'ateismo moderno* (Rome: Stadium, 1964).

harmful, like an opium that dulls the senses and distracts us from our historical responsibilities to transform the world for the better.

The referral back to independent reason as the foundation of public order also has the function of detaching the individual from tradition and from the community to which he belonged and in which he found the meaning of and nourishment for the basic moral certainties for his private and social life. The individual thus isolated from his relationships, plucked from his historical and cultural background, feels lost, out of his "element" (the *un-heimlich* of Freud and Heidegger)[17] as if he no longer had a home and nothing was really familiar to him (*heimlich*). Without acknowledged roots in a historical tradition, moral identity cannot but be formal and therefore incapable of structuring and motivating a subject for the common good of society.[18]

Yet another factor intervenes to aggravate the ethical crisis of modernity. In an antimetaphysical and reductionist context, such as that characterized by scientific unilateralism that identifies as rational only what can be tested and checked, basic moral certainties are stripped of their objective, cognitive value and thus returned to the sphere of emotions or subjective decisions. Judging a universal and objective definition of good as the foundation of morality to be impracticable, modern spokesmen for ethics understand the matter of morality as a matter of justice vis à vis one's neighbor and the right context in which to seek the rules for social collaboration.[19]

As a consequence practical rationality will be reduced either to a careful calculation of the pros and cons of a certain course of action (*proportionalism*), or else it will look for procedural criteria to guarantee the formal equality of opportunities between participants in a

17. Graziella Berto, *Freud, Heidegger lo spaesamento* (Milan: Bompiani, 2002).

18. It is hardly necessary to give, in this respect, the example of the lack of any mention of the Christian roots of Europe in the preamble of the Constitution, signed in Rome on October 29, 2004.

19. Livio Melina, Juan-Jose Perez-Soba, and Daniel Granada, *Limiti alla responsabilità? Amore e giustizia* (Rome: Lateran University Press, 2005).

hypothetical public debate, for the purposes of a fair decision (*proceduralism*). In both cases the inadequacy of the approach as a means of accounting for moral experience with all its factors is obvious, as is the loss of the original dimension of moral knowledge that it causes, which does not involve calculating the most advantageous course of action, nor respecting the opinion of the majority, but rather the irreducible difference between good and evil, that unconditionally challenges the conscience as the condition for the truth of the subject who acts.[20] "For what is a man profited, if he shall gain the whole world, and lose his own soul?" (Matthew 16:26). Consideration of solely formal rules in the definition of justice leaves the rights of those who are a minority, of those who have no voice or have no way of making their voice heard, without protection.

At the beginning of its history, modernity did not intend to change the contents of Christian morality, but only to make them independent of any reference to faith, by basing them on pure reason. In actual fact history has shown what a mistake it is to think that we can forgo a religious view of reality without thereby losing something we would not wish to renounce, because we could not do without it.[21] Detached from Christian revelation and separated from their foundation in God, Christian moral values gradually lose their certainty, to such an extent that it becomes impossible to uphold them in such a radically secularized context.

This is the case for the concept of the "dignity" of the human being, which underpins all those "human rights" so characteristic of the modern language of public ethics.[22] The idea of human dignity is far older than that of human rights: indicating a simple quality of an in-

---

20. Juan-Jose Perez-Soba, "La experiencia moral," in *Una luz para el obrar. Experiencia moral, caridad y acción cristiana,* ed. L. Melina, J. Noriega, and J.-J. Perez-Soba (Madrid: Ediciones Palabra, 2006), 29–48.

21. Please read the lucid arguments put forward by Romano Guardini, *Das Ende der Neuzeit. Ein Versuch zur Orientierung* (Munich: Katholische Akademie, 1984).

22. Robert Spaemann, "Grenzen. Zur ethischen Dimension des Handelns," *Über den Begriff der Menschenwürde* (Stuttgart: Klett-Cotta Verlag, 2001), 107–22.

tuitive nature, something undefinable. According to the well-known Kantian argument, a "thing" has a price, because it can always be substituted by another thing, while a "person" possesses dignity, precisely because as a moral subject who is unique and unrepeatable he can never be replaced.[23] The notion of dignity implies something sacred that pertains to the human person, something that is not open to manipulation, something that cannot be reduced to a "thing" of which one could make use because one owns it.[24] Although extremely fragile and exposed to multiple threats, the life of a human person nevertheless possesses an inviolable dignity in reference to the freedom of others. Horkheimer and Adorno show that they have understood this very well indeed when they write that in actual fact the only argument against homicide is a religious one.[25]

The Judeo-Christian Revelation undoubtedly contributed to the evidence of the dignity of the human being as a unique and unrepeatable person when it spoke of the unique relationship in which each person finds himself with the God who calls him by name. In effect, Greek thought which together with Plato was able to analyze so marvellously the greatness of the human spirit that was open to truth, had no moral difficulty in allowing the killing of defective newborn babies.[26] The singular dignity of each person, over and above nature and even the people to whom he belongs, emerges clearly when Christianity reveals that every human being is called to communion with God in eternal life. When, on the contrary, this light is obscured or rejected, perception of the inviolable dignity of every human person from his conception to the natural end of his days becomes inevitably dimmer. If the human being is nothing but the realization of a specific

23. Immanuel Kant, *Groundwork of a Metaphysics of Morals,* trans. C. M. Korsgaard (Cambridge: Cambridge University Press, 2012).

24. Robert Spaemann, *Personen. Versuche über den Unterschied zwischen "etwas" und "jemand"* (Stuttgart: Klett-Cotta, 1996).

25. Max Horkheimer, and Theodor Adorno, *Dialektik der Aufklärung* (Frankfurt: Suhrkamp, 1942).

26. Plato, *The Republic,* vol. 6, trans. Allan Bloom (Jackson: Basic Books, 1968).

nature that can be substituted, if he is simply an example of a species, then nature and the species are worth more than the individual, and the individual can and should be subordinated and possibly even sacrificed for the common good.

At the end of the second part of our reflection we may draw a further conclusion. When the moral life of our Western societies dares to establish itself independently of any reference to God, and deliberately breaks away from its Christian roots, it will see the signs of those principles that should guide our actions for the common good, become fainter. Claiming human rights in such a context of relativism leaves them without a proper basis and becomes a claim for the respect of formal rules, which in the final analysis only protect the strongest, those who are able to make their voices heard.

Pascal's Suggestion and Benedict's Way

Scientific progress and the demand for human rights are the conquests of human civilization, of which nobody would deny the value or which no one would seriously consider renouncing. They were born in the context of a civilization that recognized the intrinsic rationality of what is real and the specific dignity of the human being, and based them on the idea of God the Creator. On the other hand, scientism and individualism, which constitute the context of the secularization that followed, deny the very foundation of these conquests and so run the risk of turning them against man. In one respect the denial of the existence of a Logos, the Creator of being and of the good, makes the arguments of science and ethics self-contradictory. Moreover, in the light of such a denial, and confronted with the new challenges of the present, praxis is left without any adequate guidance, and risks rising up against man.

After having examined how the eclipse of the sense of God involves a corresponding eclipse of man, the time has now come to look for some positive line. But how to find a way for a possible dialogue between modern rationality and the knowledge faith possesses within the situation just described? Obviously it would be illusory to think we could return to the old pre-Galilean alliance of a total and harmonious body of knowledge. "Paradise is lost to him who has eaten of the tree of knowledge."[27] However, it is more necessary than ever to establish a correlation that will enable the horizon of rationality to be widened so as to insert scientific thinking and moral reflection in the context of that knowledge of man that still leaves some room for the reference to God and to his possible revelation.

This is where we allow ourselves to be guided by the indications offered first by the theologian Cardinal Joseph Ratzinger and then by Pope Benedict XVI. Taking up a suggestion made by the great Blaise Pascal to his nonbeliever friends,[28] he invited them to "in any case endeavour to live and conduct their lives *veluti si Deus daretur*, as if there were a God."[29] As we see, Grotius's hypothesis, which is at the beginning of modernity, is thus turned upside-down, and this on the basis of a way of thinking that actually belongs to modernity and that intends to keep the way to mystery open through actual practice. Along these lines, Pope Benedict has advised us to "open the spaces of rationality wider to the great questions of what is true and good, thus combining theology, philosophy and the sciences with each other, fully respecting each one's methods and autonomy, but also aware of the intrinsic unity that keeps them together."[30]

The first major question that this suggestion involves is overcoming a narrow idea of reason that identifies it with the method and requirements of empirical science. Reason is not a measure to be imposed on things so as to rip out their secrets and manipulate them, but openness to reality including all its factors. And since reality ap-

27. Pera, "Introduzione," 20.

28. Blaise Pascal, *Pensées*, ed. Leon Brunschvicg (Paris: Hachette, 1905), 230–41.

29. J. Ratzinger, "La crisi delle culture," in *L'Europa di Benedetto*, 62–63.

30. Benedict XVI, *Address to the Participants of the IV National Convention of the Italian Church* (Verona, 2006). The invitation was echoed by the pope in his famous *Address to the University of Regensburg* (September 12, 2006).

pears in a multiplicity of dimensions, reason will have to express itself in many different approaches and methods in order to grasp it, without forcing it into the unilateralism of a single method, effective for "measurable quantities," but unable to grasp anything that goes beyond what is visible.

The exclusion of knowledge from all that exceeds the grasp of what can be empirically tested has led to a mechanistic and materialistic consideration of the world, which renders it prey to manipulation at will. The recognition of the dazzling prospects opened up by technology has, however, been accompanied in recent times by a more acute perception of the risks in such a concept as well, in terms of ecological destruction of the planet and the arbitrary and perturbing manipulations on the part of an anonymous and uncontrolled power. We have become aware of certain dimensions of reality that are neglected and not properly known: the world is not merely material for indiscriminate use. It contains within itself a "logos" that has to be recognized and respected. The rationality of sciences is asking to be modeled on the rationality of a more comprehensive knowledge that is able to be in harmony with the meanings that the Logos of the Creator has written in the creatures.

Christianity offers human reason the revelation that the Logos is also Agape, love that is communicated and given to creatures. The vision of reality that embraces the hypothesis of creation implies the idea of an immanent meaning in completed reality. Every creature is made up of the relationship with the Creator right unto his very being. Therefore he is not outside it like the clockmaker who remains outside the mechanism that he has built and which can now function even without him. Creation appears like a gift in a mutual transport of love whereby the Giver stamps his direction upon the very being of the creature, and remains intimately present.[31] Consequently, the significance of each creature can only be grasped within the established

31. Kenneth Schmitz, *The Gift: Creation* (Milwaukee: Marquette University Press, 1982).

relationship it has with the Creator, in a train of logic that is never the mere affirmation of the separate identity of the other creatures, but expresses itself as love within the irreducible difference of self from the other.[32]

This emerges above all in the world of persons and in reference to Jesus Christ. His being, as the second Person of the Holy Trinity, a relationship that exists with the Father in the Holy Spirit, should not be understood as an ontological exception, but as the key that allows us to understand the very nature of man: it is the relationship that actually reveals the deepest significance of being a person.[33] Therefore in every human being there is an inborn call to form a communion of persons, in the image of the Holy Trinity.

Following this line of thought, it is even possible to realize how the moral rationality of public life is better ensured in the hypothesis of the acknowledgment of God. The insistence on the right of individuals to liberty, which is typical of modernity, stands without an adequate foundation if we lose the certainty of the irreducible dignity of every single person. Moreover, it risks dissolving society in the absence of a concept of the common good. Accepting Pope Benedict's proposal allows us to glimpse paths toward a solution in regard to both sides of the challenge of today.

With regard to the first question, that about the foundation of human rights: opposing the quantitative and opportunistic logic that aims at scientifically organizing the subjective well-being of the greatest number of individuals, the idea that human dignity has to be respected always and everywhere might appear archaic and counterproductive. For the single human being not to be considered merely the example of a species that can perhaps be sacrificed in an opportunistic calculation of pros and cons, the requirement of absolute and unconditional respect has to be anchored to what is absolute and un-

32. Schindler, *Heart of the World*, 196–99.

33. Joseph Ratzinger, "Zum Personenverstandis in der Theologie," in *Dogma und Verkündigung* (Wewel Verlag, 1977).

conditional, like God's initiative that wanted each person for himself, and at the same time called him to communion with him in eternity.

Second, it is becoming increasingly clear that we need to rediscover the sense of a common good in our societies, so that citizens may feel that they are part of social life. Aside from merely formal justice that defends the individual's right to liberty by placing limits on interference from others and the state, it is a matter of recognizing that only inside communal life is the true good of every single person possible.[34] In Plato's *Gorgias*, Socrates points out that the common good is not only the result of a compromise of interests that lasts for as long as there is a balance of forces, but that it is in the specific interest of every reasonable man: "when good comes to light, it is common to all."[35] This coming to light of the common good is the work of the "logos," that prevails over the antagonism of the various different individual interests with the superior convenience of the communion of persons. However, for this to happen, the other with his individual rights should not be for me only a limit to respect, or an object defined solely in relation to my subjectivity. There has to be love, namely, that attitude that enables a person to recognize the reality of the other as being in itself worthy of affirmation.[36] That man has no price, but does have dignity, ultimately signifies that his existence, as a manifestation of the Absolute, is good in itself and worthy of being loved. Thus, even in the deepest foundation of common good there is acceptance of an authority that is the basis of the intrinsic value of every human being and the goodness of the reciprocal relationship.

---

34. Alasdaire MacIntyre, *Dependent Rational Animals: Why Human Beings Need the Virtues* (Chicago: Open Court, 1999), 97–116.

35. Plato, *Gorgias*, trans. Benjamin Jowett (Rockville: Serenity Publishers, 2009).

36. Benedict XVI, *Deus Caritas Est* [God Is Love], 6; see also J. Noriega, "The Spark of Sentiment and the Fullness of Love," in *The Way of Love: Reflections on Pope Benedict XVI's Encyclical Deus Caritas Est*, ed. Livio Melina and Carl Anderson (San Francisco: Ignatius Press, 2006), 287–99.

Conclusion

To the voice that always seeks man, "Adam, where are you?" the Virgin Mary answers the angel fully, "Here am I!" (Luke 1:38). Her reply of total willingness in the face of something that surpasses reason is itself utterly reasonable. Mary knows that beyond what can be seen and measured with our senses and reason, the God of our Fathers is faithful and trustworthy. Therefore she opens her mind and heart, her very life, to welcome a greater "Logos," which is likewise love.

The reference to Mary is not merely an indication of devotion; it invites us to grasp that structural dimension of human reason, which makes it true when faced with mystery: the willing openness that offers room for a rationality greater than our own. If Grotius's hypothesis caused the eclipse of man, then Benedict's proposal to reverse it and think and live "as if God existed" might enable man to find himself again.

four

Hadley Arkes

THAT "INTELLIGENT SUPERINTENDING PRINCIPLE"

*The Author of the Rights That Were There before the
Constitution and the Bill of Rights*

I take, as my opening portion of text, that admonition sagely offered by G. K. Chesterton when he remarked on those people who
come to love one strand in Catholicism more than they love Catholicism itself. And that produces, in each case, a notable disfiguring. If
they come to appreciate a soul, apart from our bodily existence, they
may cultivate a contempt for the body and for life. They neglect the
cardinal point that we are souls embodied, that bodily life is a good,
that death does not stand on the same plane as life as a good to be
chosen; and so they may fall into rituals of collective suicide, all done
in the name of the "spiritual life." As Chesterton put it, this person

takes one idea out of the thousandfold throng of Catholic ideas; and announces that he cares for that Catholic idea more than for Catholicism. He takes it away with him into a wilderness, where the idea becomes an image and the image an idol. Then, after a century or two, he suddenly wakes up and discovers that the idol is an idol; and, shortly after that, that the wilderness is a wilderness. If he is a wise man, he calls himself a fool. If he is a fool, he calls himself an evolutionary progressive.[1]

What brought all of this to mind was a letter from a friend at another university. I had spoken at his place on Constitution Day and used the occasion to recall the serious argument, at the beginning of the Constitution, on the wisdom of adding a Bill of Rights. That there was a serious argument seems to come as news even to many lawyers and judges. And the philosophic concern seems to be no less surprising: The concern among some of the Founders, such as James Wilson and Alexander Hamilton, was that a Bill of Rights would misinstruct the American people about the ground of their rights. It would impart the sense that the rights that were mentioned, or written down in the text, were somehow more fundamental, more logically prior, than the rights that the Framers had neglected to set down. It would also impart the sense that these rights were rights of the positive law—the law that was posited, set down, enacted in any place by the men who could expect to have their commands treated as binding edicts, with a claim to be regarded as law. And do we not find the evidence all about us, as in that familiar line, heard quite often, when people invoke those rights they have "through the First Amendment." Do they imply that in the absence of that amendment they would not have had those rights to speak and assemble? As the crusty Theodore Sedgwick put it, in the House of Representatives, during that original debate about a bill of rights, Why would you suppose that in a regime of liberty, a regime of freedom, people would not have a presumptive right

1. "The Thing: ... Why I Am a Catholic," in *The Collected Works of G. K. Chesterton,* vol. 3 (San Francisco: Ignatius Press, 1990), 317.

to speak and to assemble for a discussion? Why not go on, he said, to specify our right to get up in the morning, our right to walk down the street, our right to wear a hat?[2]

My friend at another university raised a familiar question in retort: Wouldn't that right to speak, however, to engage in criticism of the government and debate over the laws—wouldn't that freedom to speak be far more central or fundamental than other rights? At the risk of straining the analogy, I would linger with that notion of *taking one strand detached from all of the rest*—for we run the risk now of losing the larger cluster of principles, the character of the regime, its animating principles, and the way in which those principles are made operational in the legal structure—we run the risk of imparting an outsized significance to any of the parts and losing our sense of the whole that informs and imparts meaning to the separate strands.

Let me work my way from the smaller connections back to that larger design of the whole. The point has been aptly made that the provisions, in the First Amendment, on the freedom of speech and of the press presuppose an economy with property in private hands. If the government owned the printing presses, if nothing could be published without the approval of people in political power, the provisions on free speech and the press would be words without substance. In Chile, under Allende, the government simply used its enlarging powers over the economy to withhold newsprint from the opposition press, as a way of silencing the critics without even the need for laws imposing censorship and explicit constraints. (Even in America, we discover that President Franklin D. Roosevelt was so vexed at the *Chicago Tribune* during the war that he was tempted to invoke the powers of the government, in commanding the economy in wartime, to withhold ink and newsprint from the *Tribune*.)

---

2. The citations to Sedgwick and the recall of that original argument over the Bill of Rights can be found in my *Beyond the Constitution* (Princeton: Princeton University Press, 1990), chap. 4, "On the Dangers of a Bill of Rights: Restating the Federalist Argument," 65–67.

The provision on freedom of speech makes sense as a restraint on the powers of government in relation to private persons and corporations. That sense of a private sphere, marked by private property, not immediately under the control of the government, may be as important as the notion of speaking in marking the character of the regime in which the freedom to speak finds its place. Of course, the freedom of speech does not mean that people may not inflict serious injuries through the use of speech, and that, when they do, that the law is incapable of punishing that speech. As John Marshall put it, in the early days of the republic, anyone who publishes a libel in this country may be *sued or indicted*—he may be prosecuted for a criminal offense if no injured party comes forth to explain, or he may be sued in an action for personal damages sustained by his victims.[3] The First Amendment implied a restraint distinctly *on the government* acting through the powers of law to silence critics. But it also depended critically on the assumption that we had access to principles of judgment in distinguishing the rightful from the wrongful uses of speech—distinguishing, that is, the cases in which the restraint on speech would be eminently justified and the cases in which it would be unjustified. We have little trouble, in that vein, telling the difference between an upsetting call, conveying news of a death in the family, and an obscene call, carried out for the purpose of tormenting, instilling fear, for no higher purpose than the satisfaction of the caller. There are some people in our own day, found chiefly in the American Civil Liberties Union (ACLU), who contend that the case for freedom of speech is anchored in the premise that there are in fact no moral truths, and no grounds on which to make these discriminations between the speech that is legitimate or illegitimate, innocent or wrongful. Years ago I was drawn into the dispute that arose as a rag-tag bunch of self-styled Nazis sought to march through a suburban community outside Chicago,

3. John Marshall, "Address on the Constitutionality of the Alien and Sedition Acts" (December 1789), in *The Political Thought of American Statesmen,* ed. Morton Frisch and Richard Stevens (Itasca: Peacock Publishers, 1973), 99–116 at 113.

in Skokie, containing many people who had survived the death camps in Europe. In that dispute I was invited into New York by Aryeh Neier to state the other side in the argument with the ACLU. As the ACLU famously argued, the American people should have the right to hear the Nazis because they should have the right to choose the Nazis in an election. In other words, the regime of freedom begins with the notion that there are no grounds for saying that the ends of the Nazis, in rejecting constitutional government, or a regime of freedom, are any less legitimate than the ends of a party that would preserve that regime of freedom. In the moral universe of the ACLU, there is a passionate attachment to liberty unrestrained, unless it is the speech of antiabortion demonstrators. But in the reigning philosophy of this organization, committed to a high civic purpose, there are no moral grounds on which to insist that the regime of freedom and constitutional restraints has a higher claim to our respect than a regime that would deny those rights at the foundation. There is no ground, then, on which to distinguish a high civic purpose from a fraudulent purpose, offering itself as high. The First Amendment presupposes a moral understanding quite at odds with that view, and if we had the time I think we could show that the version offered by the ACLU dissolves in incoherence.

But to understand that the First Amendment presupposes a structure of objective moral truths is already to fill in something that is not apparently grasped even by many lawyers who have taken the defense of the First Amendment as their life's work, as with the lawyers of the ACLU.

My friend Robert Bork, in one of his interesting opinions as a federal judge, extended the First Amendment to cover the freedom of a sculptor in crafting a piece of sculpture. And yet, it was a serious stretch. The First Amendment, as we know, was brought forth for the sake of protecting political speech and the freedom of religion. Sculpture was not exactly among the things that the First Amendment was crafted to protect, and as the judges would follow that limited understanding, they also contrived a distinction between political speech and commercial speech. Up until the 1970s the First Amendment was not thought to cast any serious protections around commercial speech, the speech that would be used in hawking one's wares, even when one's wares happened to be discount drugs or the services of a lawyer. As the judges worked themselves out of that narrow cast, they came to understand that if it is legitimate, say, to engage in the manufacture and sale of certain drugs, it should be presumptively legitimate to use the speech that is a necessary annex to the marketing of those legitimate drugs. But all of this was an arguable stretch under the First Amendment, which was designed foremost for political speech. And yet it was not at all a stretch under the original Constitution, as understood by Federalists such as Theodore Sedgwick. For in their understanding, this was a regime of freedom, and we would have a presumptive claim to *all dimensions of our freedom*—whether we were advertising our wares, doing sculpture, or walking down the street. None of these things was insulated from the reach of the law when they were vehicles for wrongdoing—as in selling certain risky drugs without a prescription. But the premise in a regime of law is that human beings, moral agents, have the competence to deliberate about the grounds of their own well-being, and the burden falls properly to the government to justify any restrictions of that freedom. If Judge Bork could make a connection between sculpture and the First Amendment, I would pose the question of why it was not just as clear—even clearer—to make the connection between those freedoms and the anchoring premises of the Constitution in a regime of freedom—that it would make as much sense to do that as to bring things like commercial freedom under the First Amendment, where they did not readily fit.

And so what I would offer so far is that "speech" may be no different from walking down the street or leaving one's house or selling one's wares. These are all aspects of personal freedom. The restriction of any one of them, without restraint, could be quite devastating. If the government could arbitrarily command that no one leave his house, that we are in an emergency, the right to speak may be rendered innocuous, for one may not be able to assemble or to find an outlet. The government could close the wires, the government could bar people from selling their goods, and virtually remove from them the means of making a living and supporting their families. The late Aaron Director remarked that the right to speak and publish strikes intellectuals and academics as matters of unsurpassed importance. But for ordinary folk, closing the banks, barring access to their savings; imposing wage-price controls; and barring people from making a living—all of these things touch freedoms that may be, for ordinary people, the difference between existence and nonexistence.

In the same vein, we have had serious people contend that it's really the Second Amendment that is most vital to a regime of freedom: "the right of the people to keep and bear Arms, shall not be infringed." That theme has been sounded by that eminent doctor of laws, Charlton Heston. But along with him, Stephen Cates, Nelson Lund, and others remind us of the move of General Gage in Boston, in 1775, to disarm the local population.[4] A government that can disarm ordinary people deprives them of the means of protecting themselves from private assailants and from armies of occupation, committed to removing the terms of principle on which free people deserve to live.

In our own day, of course, the "first freedom," the most decisive freedom has been redefined by many people to be not the freedom of religion or of speech, but the freedom, and the right, to order an abortion. That freedom has become, for many, an anchoring right, meant to secure a large portion of freedom in matters sexual—freedom from the moral reproaches and judgments cast by others, and cast most critically in the form of laws that forbid and restrict. But we know that this move has been seen as striking because it has re-

4. See Stephen Halbrook, "The Original Understanding of the Second Amendment," in *The Bill of Rights: Original Meaning and Current Understanding*, ed. Eugene Hickock (Charlottesville: University of Virginia Press, 1991), 117–29; Nelson Lund, "Taking the Second Amendment Seriously," *Weekly Standard* (July 24, 2000), 21–16.

placed the strand of the First Amendment that really has been seen as the "first freedom." If we are to take apart strands, then there has been a powerful case made over the years for freedom of religion as the strand that truly stands as the "first freedom." (It must be said here, though, even parenthetically, that the accent on the First Amendment seems to have deflected people from that provision even more critical in the original text of the Constitution, unamended [Article VI, para. 3]: "no religious Test shall ever be required as a Qualification to any Office or public Trust under the United States.") When George Washington wrote his letter to the Jewish Congregation in Newport, Rhode Island, Jews were still not permitted the vote in that state. But in the law of the Constitution, Jews and Christians stood on the plane of a common citizenship; the United States was the only polity in the world in which that common standing could take place.

But we need to remind ourselves that the case for religion as a "first freedom" did not reside simply in a claim for tolerance. In one of his most luminous political essays, James Madison made the explicit connection between religion and a constitutional order. I refer, of course, to his "Memorial and Remonstrance against Religious Assessments" in Virginia in 1785. In our own day, people may have a view of religion so wide, so anxious to avoid invidious distinctions, that they would take in some rather vague notions of "forces at work in the universe." But as Madison and his generation understood the matter, religion involved "the duty which we owe to our Creator and the manner of discharging it." Religion involved, that is, the obligations that flowed to the Creator of the universe, the Author of those laws of nature that encompassed the distinct nature of human beings, with a capacity to reflect on moral obligations and the origin of all things. (As Chesterton once remarked, only human beings have a religious sense—when was the last time you heard of a cow giving up grass on Fridays?) The existence of that Creator and the Author of the moral laws alerted us at the very least to a law outside ourselves. As Madison put it,

It is the duty of every man to render to the Creator such homage and such only as he believes to be acceptable to him. This duty is precedent, both in order of time and in degree of obligation, to the claims of Civil Society. Before any man can be considered as a member of Civil Society, he must be considered as a subject of the Governour of the Universe: And if a member of Civil Society ... do it with a saving of his allegiance to the Universal Sovereign.[5]

The moral law, offered by that Lawgiver, was in place even before the advent of civil society, and it established then an obligation that *preceded* civil society. Or, we might say, it furnished the understanding of the moral grounds on which we committed ourselves in the first place to a regime of law. At the same time, that moral law marked limits on what the positive law in any place could rightly command. As Plato taught us, there was the most elementary distinction between a person who recognized a law outside himself and one who recognized no law beyond his own appetites. For many in that first generation, and in ours, the awareness of that moral law, and the Author of that law, furnished the moral ground for the respecting of other laws. And it supplied the ground for respecting, in the first instance, the difference between a regime of law, a regime that bound both rulers and citizens to a common law, and a despotism, a regime with no law beyond the will of the rulers. Quite apart from everything else, the absorption of that moral sense made the most profound difference for citizens in a republic. It helped to form, that is, beings who had absorbed an understanding of an obligation to respect the laws. And if we were establishing in America, for the first time, the right of a people to govern themselves, it was even more critical to cultivate in ordinary people a sense of obligation to respect the laws made by their fellow citizens, in contrast with laws propounded by princes with all of the trappings and majesty of royalty. As George Washing-

5. James Madison, "Memorial and Remonstrance against Religious Assessments," in *Selected Writings of James Madison,* ed. Ralph Ketcham (Indianapolis: Hackett, 2006), 21–27.

ton once asked, of what avail was it to have established the right of a people to govern themselves if the measures enacted by that people, in giving laws to themselves, need not be obeyed?[6]

At the same time, that religious understanding established a recognition of limits on the reach of political authority. Altogether, it was the most wholesome groundwork that could have been put in place in conveying an understanding of limited government: a government that could not be authorized to reach everything, a government that began with a sense of the moral and constitutional limits on what it could command. As Jefferson famously noted, there was, in a popular government, nothing above the rule of the majority—nothing "except the moral law." But the recognition of that law, with its governing sense of right and wrong, made all the difference between a people constituted as a political people and a criminal band.

In fact, we find that if we pursue this matter now to the root, we discover that the case for a government restrained by law is virtually the same as the understanding of a human being, properly constituted; a human being with self-control—as Plato put it, a being who has a constitutional ruler within himself. As Plato pointed out, a person with self-control is not a weaker person, and for the same reason a government under self-control, a government restrained within itself, is not a weaker government. A person under self-control understands that he does not have the right to do everything within his powers; he understands, as a moral agent, that he cannot claim the "right to do a wrong." He cannot claim, for example, a right to kill a person afflicted by deafness—or a right to kill *himself* because he is afflicted with deafness. To recognize that one has no right to do these things is to recognize the things one has no right to do even in the name of one's freedom and the governance of oneself. A person who rules out those things he has no right to do may be directed then to concentrate his

6. See George Washington, "Sixth Annual Message to Congress (November 19, 1794)" in *George Washington: A Collection,* ed. W. B. Allen (Indianapolis: Liberty Classics, 1988), 493.

powers on that range of things *rightful* for him to do. And a government focused in that way—with its own recognition of moral restraints—is a government enhanced, not weakened, in its powers, for it would now be concentrating its powers on its proper, rightful ends.

What I am pointing out, then, is that when we draw out the understanding in this way, we sketch in the moral understanding that tracks, and underlies, Chief Justice Marshall's classic opinions in *McCulloch v. Maryland* (1819) and *Marbury v. Madison* (1803), and which yields this point, not widely noticed: If we begin with that recognition of a law outside ourselves, a body of moral truths that commands our respect, we set in place the understanding that enjoins us to have a constitutional government, a regime restrained by law—*even if there were no written constitution.*

And once again, the anchor of it all, for that generation of the founding, was the awareness of that moral law, standing before civil society—and that Author of that law. But that sense of the centrality of the religious understanding brings me back to my opening theme on the Bill of Rights, and our understanding of the regime that contains these rights. My opening was to warn about the danger of misshaping our understanding as we took fragments, such as the right to speak, and detached them from that larger ensemble of principles that marked the character of the regime. In the case of the religious understanding, that matter runs beyond the inventory of rights set down— it truly does run to the core of things, as we would see if we returned for a moment to that original argument about the Bill of Rights.

As James Wilson tellingly observed, the purpose of this new government, and this new Constitution, was not to create new rights, but to secure and enlarge the rights we already possessed by nature. If we attached a codicil to the Constitution, on *the rights we had not given up,* or the natural rights we regarded then as unalienable, the assumption would come into play that we had indeed surrendered the vast body of our rights when we entered civil society and came under this new Constitution. That was indeed one construction of the "State of nature" and the transition to civil society. As Blackstone famously put it, we give up the full range of rights we possessed in the State of Nature, including, as he said, our "liberty to do mischief," and we exchange those unqualified rights for a more compressed or contracted set of rights under civil society—call them "civil rights." But those diminished rights are rendered more secure by the advent of a government that can now protect and secure those rights.

I have had the occasion to point out in another place that James Wilson responded to that argument with one of those telling Talmudic questions: When did we ever have a liberty to do mischief?[7] In other words, to translate the question into the terms of Aquinas or our own Abraham Lincoln, when did we ever have a "right to do a wrong"? If we follow the clues left us by Wilson, we would recognize that, even in the State of Nature, we never had a right to murder, to rape, to assault. And so as we entered civil society, the laws that restrained us now from murder and rape did not restrain us from anything we ever had the right, the rightful liberty, to do. What rights then did we give up when we entered this government, under this Constitution? The answer tendered by the Federalists was: none. As Alexander Hamilton put it in the Federalist no. 84, Here the people surrender nothing—they surrender none of their rights.

Again, the very purpose of the government was to secure and enlarge the protection of our natural rights, and so we don't begin with the people surrendering the vast body of their rights, named and unnamed. If we suggest that the protection of natural rights is something tacked on as an afterthought, as a codicil to the Constitution, we begin to suggest that the protection of natural rights was in fact something secondary or peripheral. And we begin to suggest that the purpose of the larger scheme, the purpose of the Constitution, was something other than the protection of natural rights. Yet what could that be? The protection of property? The cultivation of honor? Or

7. See Wilson in Arkes, "Beyond the Constitution," 63.

any other desirable thing—detached from the body of principles that marked the distinct character of this regime?

The Federalists, such as Hamilton and Wilson, can be understood here only as they rejected the moral understanding of Hobbes in his construction of the State of Nature and indeed, in his construction of the moral world. As Hobbes famously put it in the *Leviathan,* "the desires, and other passions of man are in themselves no sin. No more are the actions, that proceed from those passions, till they know a law that forbids them: which till laws be made they cannot know."[8] That is, before the existence of law and civil society, we cannot expect men to know the difference between right and wrong, or to treat that difference as one they can afford to respect. That was an understanding evidently rejected quite clearly by James Wilson in his commentaries, when he observed that we had no right to do a wrong even in the State of Nature. In other words, even in those intervals when governments break down, people living without the presence of the laws were still living in a moral world, where the moral laws were intact.

But in this vein, no one made the rebuttal of Hobbes more explicit than the nineteen-year-old Alexander Hamilton, in his revolutionary pamphlet, "The Farmer Refuted," the pamphlet written when he was still a student at King's College in New York. We are reminded what undergraduates were once capable of grasping—and explaining—in that age of rare formal schooling and high literacy. For the young Hamilton offered this account: Hobbes, he wrote, "held ... that [man in the state of nature] was ... perfectly free from all restraints of law and government. Moral obligation, according to [Hobbes], is derived from the introduction of civil society; and there is no virtue, but what is purely artificial, the mere contrivance of politicians, for the maintenance of social intercourse." And the young Hamilton was no less precise in touching, at once, the central point of corruption in the argument:

8. Thomas Hobbes, *Leviathan* (Oxford: Basil Blackwell, 1960 [1651]), 83.

The reason [Hobbes] runs into this absurd and impious doctrine, was, that he disbelieved the existence of an intelligent superintending principle, who is the governor, and will be the final judge of the universe.... Good and wise men, in all ages, have embraced a very dissimilar theory. They have supposed, that the deity, from the relation we stand in, to himself and to each other, has constituted an eternal and immutable law, which is, indispensibly, obligatory upon all mankind, *prior to any human institution whatever.*[9]

What has to be said, if we look seriously at the record, is that the references to the Creator who endowed us with rights, were no mere rhetorical flourishes, or devices to adorn the documents. They ran to the very root of the understanding about rights and the ends of the political order. The understanding of the laws of nature and of nature's God placed us within a cosmos with a moral structure. It made a profound difference in fixing the understanding that there were standards of right and wrong apart from the positive law. And it explained why those bipeds who conjugated verbs were the bearers of rights. But on that cardinal first point, James Wilson offered the argument, startling at the time, that contrary to the teachings of Locke and Blackstone, the law could indeed incorporate a principle of revolution. For Locke and Blackstone it was evident that a revolution unsettled the standing law. But Wilson, in his lectures on jurisprudence, insisted that the American law began by actually incorporating a principle of revolution. It began, that is, by recognizing the possibility that revolution could be justified because even a decent government could turn itself into a tyranny.[10] The American law began with the recognition that there could

9. See Alexander Hamilton, "The Farmer Refuted" [February 1775], in *The Papers of Alexander Hamilton,* ed. Harold C. Syrett (New York: Columbia University Press, 1961), vol. 1, 86–87 (emphasis added).

10. In his first lecture on jurisprudence, in 1790, Wilson insisted that "a revolution principle certainly is, and certainly should be taught as a principle for the constitution of the United States, and of every State in the Union." See Wilson, "First Lecture on the Law," in *The Works of James Wilson,* ed. Robert Green McCloskey (Cambridge, Mass.: Harvard University Press, 1967 [1804]), vol. 1, 79.

be an unjust law: that the positive law could be made with all of the trappings of legality, while the law itself lacked the substance of justice. But the American law could have that quality only because it began with the understanding of natural rights—it began, that is, with an understanding of objective principles of right and wrong, which could be invoked at any time to measure the rightness or wrongness of those policies enacted through the positive law.

But then what of that creature, who alone had the capacity, as Aristotle said, to do more than emit sounds to indicate pleasure or pain, but to give reasons over matters of right and wrong? Even in this age of animal liberation we do not sign labor contracts with our horses or cows, or seek the informed consent of our household pets before we authorize surgery upon them. But we continue to think that those beings who can give and understand reasons deserve to be ruled with a rendering of reasons in a regime that elicits their consent. In his Cooper Union Speech in February 1860, Lincoln referred to those black slaves who did not throw in with John Brown. Even in their ignorance, as Lincoln said—even though they were illiterate and unschooled, they could still sense that the schemes of this crazy white man would not conduce to their well-being.[11] As uneducated as they were, they were still moral agents—they were beings who had the capacity to reflect about the grounds of their well-being, and they did not deserve to be annexed to the purposes of other men without their consent.

Now that may make the case for government by consent on the lowest ground—on the capacity even of unlettered men to have a lively sense of their own self-preservation. Others have made an interesting case for deriving rights from the awareness of creatures who may be suffering serious pains and injuries. From that angle, we may speak plausibly even of animals having a certain right not to suffer

11. Lincoln, "Address at Cooper Institute, New York City (February 27, 1860)," in *The Collected Works of Abraham Lincoln*, ed. Roy P. Basler (New Brunswick, N.J.: Rutgers University Press, 1953), 541.

gratuitous pain at the hands of those beings who are moral agents, and who should know better.

But there is an enduring question as to whether we can run deeper than that and speak of beings who have an intrinsic dignity, which becomes the source in turn of rights of an intrinsic dignity that the rest of us must be obliged to respect. In my book *Natural Rights and the Right to Choose,* I recalled some of my colleagues at Amherst who had taken as their signature tune that line of Nietzsche's, amplified by Dostoyevsky, that God is dead and everything is permitted. They are people of large liberal sympathies, and when they focus on that homeless person in the gutter, the man who has broken his own life, they are still inclined to say that he has an essential dignity or even sanctity. For some of my colleagues this is sanctity without the sacred: They will speak of the importance of avoiding plagiarism regarded as a sacred obligation among academics. What they mean is that the sacred is that which elicits their strongest passions; we ourselves endow something with the standing of the sacred as we invest our passions in it. By this construal, that man in the gutter who has broken his own life has a certain sanctity only because we have conferred it upon him. That is strikingly different from the understanding revealed by Justice McLean in his dissenting opinion in the *Dred Scott* case, when he leaned in to say, You may think that black man is chattel, but he is a creature who bore "the impress of his Maker," that he was "amenable to the laws of God and man," and he was "destined to an endless existence."[12] That is to say, he has a soul, which will not decompose when his material existence comes to an end. Now my colleagues in the academy are, as I say, people of generous disposition and large natures; but even they have to admit that they cannot give the same account of the wrong of slavery, or the wrong of the Holocaust that McLean was able to give. McLean's understanding still comes closer to the understanding of most Americans, because most Americans have not detached themselves from the religious tradi-

12. *Scott v. Sandford,* 60 U.S. 393, at 550 (1857).

tion. It made a profound difference in the past when we understood that even the most diminished among us were creatures made in the image of something higher. That explained why they were bearers of rights, why they bore an intrinsic dignity that the rest of us were obliged to respect. As Chesterton once put it, the Church has never said on behalf of democracy, or said within his time, what Jefferson or Lincoln said about democracy, but "there will be a rending of all religious peace and compromise, or even the end of civilization and the world, … before the Catholic Church would admit that [even] one single moron, or one single man 'is not worth saving.'"[13] Americans are far more dubious in this age about religion, and the courts have made it more difficult to bring the language of religion into the public square. And yet we discover at every turn that our moral language, our discourse on rights and wrongs, is drawn from reservoirs running deep in our religious understanding. The language has persisted, the claims of dignity and rights, but the sources of that language have evaporated from the understanding of many of our people, if indeed our most recent generations have even been made aware of those reservoirs of religious understanding.

We must be drawn then persistently to the question, What does the heavy lifting for us then that used to be done by the God of Israel? What explains our understanding of natural rights, or unalienable rights, in the absence of that premise that we were endowed with rights by our Creator, and that everything begins with a moral law that was in place even before the Constitution and the Bill of Rights? If we ourselves were the source of sanctity, if we conferred those rights upon ourselves, then we could also remove them from ourselves. And we could remove them all the more easily from certain selected classes of people, such as unborn children, whom we no longer wish to protect. If we gave those rights to ourselves, through a flexing of our own will, then why should we not be free to alienate them, to waive

13. Chesterton, "Is Humanism a Religion?" in *The Collected Works of G. K. Chesterton*, 151.

them? Why should I not be free to order up my own death if I discover, for example, that I have a grandmother of the wrong race?

The answer, curiously and magnificently rendered in the religious tradition itself, is that we do not depend on the God of Israel for all of the heavy lifting we have to do, for he has furnished us already with the powers to bring forth the account ourselves with the nature he has fashioned and the laws that we have the wit to discern. As Aquinas said, the divine law we know through revelation, while the natural law we may know through that reasoning that is accessible to human beings as human beings. There is probably no clearer or more compelling example of natural law reasoning than that fragment I've often cited from Lincoln; that fragment he wrote imagining himself in a conversation with the owner of black slaves and putting the question of why he is justified in owning other human beings: Is it because he is less intelligent than you? Beware, for the next white man who comes along, more intelligent than you, may rightly enslave you. Is it because of color, that the lighter have the right to enslave the darker? Beware again, for the next white who comes along, lighter in complexion than you, may enslave you.[14] As Lincoln continued in this vein, the upshot was that there was nothing one could cite to justify the enslavement of the black man that would not apply to many whites as well. And some of us have used the same form of argument on the matter of abortion: Why would you regard that being in the womb as anything less than a human being? It doesn't speak yet? Neither do deaf mutes? It has no arms or legs? Other people have been born missing limbs, or they lose limbs in the course of their lives without losing anything necessary to their standing, as human beings, to receive the protections of the law. And here the upshot is that there is nothing one could cite to disqualify the unborn child as a human being that would not apply to many people walking about, well outside the womb.

Now I'd point out that nothing in this chain of reasoning involves

14. See *The Collected Works of Abraham Lincoln*, vol. 2, 222–23.

an appeal to revelation. It is a model, as I say, of principled reasoning, and it is, on its own terms, accessible to people across the religious divide. It can be understood by Baptists as well as Catholics, it can be understood by people without a college education. In other words, one doesn't have to be Catholic in order to understand this argument on abortion—and that has been precisely the teaching of the Church, that this is a matter of that reasoning that is natural, accessible to human beings as human beings. And this has ever been the case in the grand arguments over natural rights, as it was during our own revolution. There is probably no clearer example on this head than that sermon delivered by the Reverend Samuel Cooper on the day that the new Constitution of Massachusetts was inaugurated in October 1780. The Reverend Cooper drew on that understanding in Paul, that we do not need revelation at every point, that we may be attentive to all of the evidence put before us, plainly in sight, and open to our reason. As the Reverend Cooper put it:

> We want not, indeed, a special revelation from heaven to teach us that men are born equal and free; that no man has a natural claim of dominion over his neighbours, not one nation any such claim upon another; and that as government is only the administration of the affairs of a number of men combined for their own security and happiness, such a society have a right freely to determine by whom and in what manner their own affairs shall be administered. These are the plain dictates of that reason and common sense with which the common parent of men has informed the human bosom.[15]

And yet, and yet: It is one thing to say that no man is by nature the ruler of other men in the way that men are by nature the rulers of dogs and horses. It is quite another to say that each person around us, no matter how diminished in his capacities, or deficient in character, has some essential, intrinsic dignity that the rest of us must be obliged to respect.

15. See Cooper's sermon in Ellis Sandoz, ed., *Political Sermons of the American Founding Era, 1730–85* (Indianapolis: Liberty Press, 1991), 629–56 at 637.

A telling test here, on this point, rang in for me a few years ago during a talk I was doing at Villanova. One student, after listening to me discourse, remarked that, in his own experience, people were driven in their motives mainly by self-interest—rather than these hifallutin' notions that I was retailing. And he asked me what I would say to that. I said that I would want to know something more about him then, to draw him out on that subject: I invited him to cast his gaze around the room, containing about seventy-five to one hundred students, and I asked him whether he agreed with Jaffa, that these people around him bore an intrinsic dignity, the source of rights of an intrinsic dignity that he was obliged to respect? Or did he regard himself as fully willing to give the ascendance, as he said, to self-interest, and regard himself as wholly free to sell these people out—to sacrifice their freedom *and even their lives*—as it suited his interests? I remarked that his answer to that question had to have the most profound bearing on the question of whether I would think it justified or even safe to share with him the power over my life by sharing with him the right to vote in shaping the government and the laws. (The questions elicited one of the rarest reactions I've ever encountered: His face reflected a certain recognition and he responded, with a smile, "Thank you.")

The firefighters on 9/11, poised at the threshold of the World Trade Center, wove into their lives the assumption that every soul they could reach in those buildings they were equally obliged to save. Once again, we could understand that point more readily when we believed that humans were made in the image of something higher. But can reason furnish itself the materials of that understanding?

My dear friend Robert George at Princeton stands, at once, as a serious Catholic and serious philosopher, and he has insisted that there is no need to make the appeal to revelation on this, the most critical point at the root of political life. His own approach to this problem puts the accent on creatures "of this nature." The human embryo is not in a position to exercise the capacities that are built into its nature as a human being. It does no syllogisms, it shows no penetrating insight or arresting wisdom; nor does it show bravery, or a willingness to subordinate its inclinations out of a respect for moral obligations. But we would not put this embryo into a soup even if it would make the soup more interesting. As unprepossessing as the embryo is, even people not very reflective will have a sense that that "is not what it is made for." It is not so trifling that it belongs in salads or soups, or deserves to be treated on the plane of ordinary animal matter. There is something of immeasurable depth contained in that smallest of beings, which is far yet even from looking the way human beings typically look. When we see beings of that kind in a maturity of competence, we recognize that they should not be governed without their consent. When we see beings of that kind, too young, or too infirm to be in command of their powers, we are summoned to treat them with a special care, and to be in awe yet of what they are, even if they are diminished in their powers.

Professor George may be quite right, and we may say enough, in explaining the ground of "natural rights," the rights that are grounded in the enduring nature of humans, by appealing mainly to the understanding of creatures of this nature—much in the way that Immanuel Kant would contend that any proposition with standing of a real moral principle could be drawn from the very idea of "a rational creature as such." And yet, does that understanding carry us over to an understanding of sanctity? Does it carry us to the understanding, as Chesterton says, that even the least among us has a life worth respecting?

We may come here to that point at which our religious tradition is so woven in with the tradition of moral philosophy that they become difficult, even impossible, at a certain point, to disentangle. The Church has become the main enclave in our own time to sustain natural law reasoning, even after the schools of philosophy have grown skeptical that reason has any serious claim to the knowledge of moral truths. And might it not have been the Church that preserved the tradition of philosophy, just as it brought forth and sustained universities, in the Middle Ages? John Paul II and his successor, Benedict, have forcefully drawn us back to remind us of the connection between the Church and Greek philosophy, from the first days of the Church. The connection was not adventitious or accidental, but quite central and necessary even at the beginning. As John Paul II had so arrestingly put it, the Church has always moved with two wings, with reason and faith. When St. Paul undertook his mission to Athens, he entered into discussions with "certain Epicurean and Stoic philosophers." When he reached outside the circle of Jews, he could not appeal to Moses and the prophets. He had to appeal to an understanding more widely accessible; as John Paul II recalled, he had to appeal to "the natural knowledge of God and to the voice of conscience in every human being."[16] Here the Fathers of the Church would build on the achievements of the Greek philosophers. For Greek religion had been polytheistic, with a persisting inclination then, as John Paul II noted, to "divinizing natural things and phenomena." But it was the considerable service of the "fathers of philosophy to bring to light the link between reason and religion":

> As they broadened their view to include universal principles, they no longer rested content with the ancient myths, but wanted to provide a rational foundation for their belief in the divinity. This opened a path which took its rise from ancient traditions but allowed a development satisfying the demands of universal reason. This development sought to acquire a critical awareness of what they believed in, and the concept of divinity was the prime beneficiary of this. Superstitions were recognized for what they were and religion was, at least in part, purified by rational analysis. It was on this basis that the Fathers of the Church entered into fruitful dialogue with ancient philosophy, which offered new ways of proclaiming and understanding the God of Jesus Christ.[17]

Greek philosophy became a powerful lever in fending off sophistry, and so it could become, as John Paul II recalled, "the hedge and

16. *Fides et Ratio*, sec. 36.
17. Ibid.

protective wall around the vineyard" of the Church. As John Paul II put it so tellingly in *Fides et Ratio*, a faith deprived of reason runs the risk of falling into feeling and sentiment, and "so runs the risk of no longer being a universal proposition." It was an illusion then, he said, to "think that faith, tied to weak reasoning, might be more penetrating; on the contrary, faith then runs the grave risk of withering into myth or superstition."[18]

Several years ago Cardinal Lustiger came in from Paris to do the Erasmus Lecture for us in New York under the Institute for Religion and Public Life. In the course of his lecture the cardinal touched on that aphorism of John Stuart Mill's that has become a reigning slogan of what has been called "liberal" philosophy: that my personal freedom finds its limit at the point at which I begin to inflict injuries on other people. Cardinal Lustiger raised the question: Do we assume that this principle covers any other person? All other persons? Do we assume that everyone out there counts, including people whose identity and character we could not know? Would it be plausible to alter that liberal slogan to make it read in this way: Our liberty ends as soon as we begin to injure, or affect adversely, those persons *who count*? And with a wink we may grasp just who doesn't count. In the middle of the nineteenth century in America, they were black people, and in our own time, as Judge Casey's queries made clear recently in New York, unborn children. (Casey asked the practitioners of partial-birth abortion just why they didn't administer an anesthetic to the child, with most of its body dangling outside the birth canal, before the surgeon punctured her head and drew out the contents of the skull. The question evidently surprised the witnesses as their reaction astonished the judge: it just never occurred to them to administer an anesthetic, for they had apparently absorbed the understanding that that being in the womb, now emerging from the womb, simply did not count. The pains and injuries sustained by that child was simply not a matter of consequence, which claimed the concern of any actor

18. Ibid., sec. 48.

in the scene.) What Lustiger was pointing out then was this: Even the most familiar cliché of liberalism had apparently absorbed the premise that "all men are created equal." But if that proposition, as Lincoln called it, was not a truth—and important segments of liberal opinion denied, after all, that this or any proposition could constitute a moral truth—if that proposition was no truth, then the most elementary dogmas of liberalism dissolve in their meaning. And of course the next question would be: Can liberalism itself account for why we would ascribe moral worth to every person, even without knowing who that person is?

The answer was wholly explicable when it was said in the past that they are all children of God, or as Locke put it, that we are "all the workmanship of one … wise Maker, … sharing in one community of nature, and there cannot be supposed any such subordination among us that may authorize us to destroy one another, as if we were made for one another's uses as the inferior ranks of creatures are made for ours."[19]

But as we trace things out in this way, I wonder if we simply come to the simple, inescapable truth of the compound we are—we are souls embodied, we are the only creatures with a religious sense, just as we are the only creatures that can bring forth law and moral judgment. No one who tries to give an account of the ground of polity and laws, no one who tries to give an account of this Constitution, can do that without, very quickly, running into the kinds of questions posed by Cardinal Lustiger, or posed even by the firefighters if they paused at the threshold to the World Trade Center and asked, Just why *are* *we* obliged to save any soul we can reach? They are the questions that cannot be evaded then by anyone who tries to explain why these human beings are the bearers of rights, and why they are destined then, by nature, as Aristotle said, to live in a *polis*. We cannot give an account then of this Constitution, or the most elementary things in our law, without drawing us back to the nature of that being who is both

19. John Locke, *Second Treatise on Civil Government* [1690], bk. 1, ch. 2, sec. 6.

the subject and object of the laws. And we cannot give an account of that being without drawing upon the mysteries running deep in that nature—like the mystery of why we have that capacity that the Greeks called *epistemonikon,* the capacity to grasp universals, along with propositions, like the law of contradiction, not bounded by space or time. It is the very capacity that made the human understanding, as Aristotle said, approach the divine. If we were made in the image of God, it was not because God had arms or legs or suffered from the maladies that afflict our bodies. It was the gift of reason that brought us closer than anything to the Mind of the One who made us. At the core then of politics, at the ground of our understanding of religion and the law, everything may finally come down to that angle on human person offered by Kant: that we are dealing here with a being who carries a metaphysic within himself.

five

~)

Robert P. George

ON THE MORAL PURPOSES OF LAW
AND THE STATE

First Principles and Contemporary Issues

The obligations and justifying purposes of law and government
are to protect public health, safety, and morals, and to advance the
general welfare—including, preeminently, protecting people's fundamental rights and basic liberties.

At first blush, this classic formulation (or combination of classic
formulations) of the purposes and powers of government seems to
accord to public authority vast and sweeping powers. Yet, in truth,
the general welfare (or common good) requires that government be
limited. Although government's responsibility is primary in respect
of defending the nation from attack and subversion, protecting peo-

ple from physical assaults and various other forms of depredation, and maintaining public order, its role is otherwise *subsidiary*: to support the work of the families, religious communities, and other institutions of civil society that shoulder the primary burden of forming upright and decent citizens, caring for those in need, encouraging people to meet their responsibilities to one another, and discouraging them from harming themselves or others.

Governmental respect for individual freedom and the autonomy of nongovernmental spheres of authority is, then, a requirement of political morality. Government must not try to run people's lives or usurp the roles and responsibilities of families, religious bodies, and other character- and culture-forming authoritative communities. The governmental usurpation of the just authority of families, religious communities, and other nongovernmental institutions is unjust in principle, often seriously so, and the record of big government in the twentieth century—even when it has not degenerated into vicious totalitarianism—shows that it does little good in the long run and frequently harms those it seeks to help.

Limited government is a key tenet of classic liberalism—the liberalism of people like Madison and Tocqueville—though today it is regarded as a conservative ideal. So perhaps those of us who continue to subscribe to the principle of limited government should think of ourselves as conservative liberals, though of course labels are of little importance. In any event, someone who believes in limited government need not embrace libertarianism, despite the fact that some hard-core libertarians hold that anyone who is prepared to acknowledge any role for government beyond preventing unjust coercion and fraud is no true friend of limited government or individual freedom. The strict libertarian position, it seems to me, goes much too far in depriving government of even its subsidiary role. It underestimates the importance of maintaining a reasonably healthy moral ecology, especially for the rearing of children, and it fails to appreciate the legitimate, albeit once again limited, role of law and government in maintaining such an ecology. (I have developed and defended this point in my book *Making Men Moral: Civil Liberties and Public Morality* and in my lecture entitled "The Concept of Public Morality," which I first presented at the Cosmos Club in a lecture series sponsored by the Institute for the Psychological Science a few years ago. I won't rehearse my arguments here.)[1]

Even those of us who are critical of strict libertarianism, however, must acknowledge that it responds to certain truths that have come increasingly into focus as experiments with big government, especially in its bureaucratic and managerial dimensions, have produced their disappointing—and sometimes deplorable—results. Command economies cannot generate economic growth and the material social benefits associated with growth, including the social mobility that enables sons of tailors to become engineers and sons of railroad workers and coal miners to become owners and developers of commercial real estate. Free markets, by contrast, if properly regulated to prevent exploitation, are engines of economic growth, social mobility, and general prosperity. Economic freedom cannot guarantee political liberty or respect for democratic political rights and the just autonomy of the institutions of civil society—the example of contemporary China seems to show this—but in the absence of economic liberty other honorable personal and institutional freedoms are rarely secure. Moreover, the concentration of economic power in the hands of government is something every true friend of civil liberties should, by now, have learned to fear.

But there is an even deeper truth—one going beyond economics—to which libertarianism responds: law and government exist to protect human persons and secure their well-being. It is not the other way round, as communist and other forms of collectivist ideology

1. *Making Men Moral: Civil Liberties and Public Morality* (Oxford: Oxford University Press, 1995); "The Concept of Public Morality," in *The Person and the Polis: Faith and Values within the Secular State*, ed. Craig Steven Titus (Arlington, Va: The Institute for the Psychological Sciences Press, 2006), 55–74.

suppose. Individuals are not cogs in a wheel. Stringent norms of political justice forbid persons to be treated as mere servants or instrumentalities of the state. These norms equally exclude the sacrificing of the dignity and rights of persons for the sake of some supposed "greater overall good."

But since we are going back to first principles, it is in season to ask: *Why not* subordinate the individual to the ends of the collectivity or the state?

Here we see how profound is the mistake of supposing that the principle of limited government and the obligation of governments to respect basic rights and liberties are rooted in the denial of moral truth or a putative requirement of governments to refrain from acting on the basis of judgments of moral truth. For our commitment to limited government and individual freedom is itself the fruit of moral conviction—conviction ultimately founded upon truths that our nation's Founders proclaimed as self-evident: namely "that all men are created equal, that they are endowed by their Creator with certain unalienable rights, and among these are life, liberty, and the pursuit of happiness."

At the very foundation of our political and ethical creed is the proposition that each human being possesses a profound, inherent, and equal dignity simply by virtue of his humanity, that is, his nature as a rational creature—a creature possessing, albeit in limited measure and in the case of some human beings merely in root or rudimentary form, the Godlike powers of reason and freedom. This great truth of natural law, which is at the heart of our civilizational and civic order, has its theological expression in the biblical teaching that man, unlike the brute animals, is made in the very image and likeness of the divine Creator and ruler of the universe.

In the domain of practical politics, it is critical to bear this great truth in mind. We must not adopt a merely pragmatic understanding or speak only of practical considerations in addressing the pressing issues of our day, including such morally controversial and socially

divisive issues as abortion, embryo-destructive stem-cell research, euthanasia, cloning, and marriage. These are inescapably moral issues,
and though they have practical aspects, they cannot be adequately understood or rightly resolved in the absence of moral reflection
and argument. Sound positions on the issues cannot be effectively advanced and defended by citizens and statesmen who are unwilling or
unable to engage moral arguments and make the moral case. That is
why we should, in my opinion, rededicate ourselves to understanding and making the moral argument for the sanctity of human life in
all stages and conditions, and the dignity of marriage as the conjugal
union of one man and one woman.

Please do not misunderstand me. I am not saying that practical
considerations should or even can be left out of the argument. In a
proper understanding of morality, practical considerations are not
"merely" practical. The moral case for the reform of unilateral-divorce
laws, for example, includes reference to the devastating social consequences of the collapse of a healthy marriage culture and the role of
unilateral divorce in contributing to the collapse. The moral argument
for restoring legal protection to the unborn includes reference to the
adverse psychological, and, in some cases, physical consequences of
abortion on many women who undergo the procedure.

Our task should be to understand the moral truth and speak it
in season and out of season. We will be told by the pure pragmatists
that the public is too far gone in moral relativism or even moral delin-
quency to be reached by moral argument. We will be advised to make
the moral arguments to the social-conservative "base" but to frame
those arguments in coded language so as not to scare off the "soc-
cer moms" or whoever is playing their role in the next election cycle.
All of this must be resisted. We must, to be sure, avoid stridency. We
must, to be sure, practice the much-neglected and badly underrated
virtue of prudence. But we must have faith that truth is luminously
powerful: so that if we bear witness to the truth about, say, marriage
and the sanctity of human life—lovingly, civilly, but also passionately

and with determination—and if we honor the truth in advancing our positions, then even many of our fellow citizens who now find themselves on the other side of these issues will—some sooner, some later—come around.

To speak of truth frightens some people today. They evidently believe that people who claim to know the truth about anything—and especially about moral matters—are "fundamentalists" and potential totalitarians. But this is silly. As Hadley Arkes has patiently explained, those on the other side of the great debates over social issues such as abortion and marriage make truth claims—moral truth claims—all the time. They assert their positions with no less confidence and no more doubt than one finds in the advocacy of pro-lifers and defenders of conjugal marriage. They proclaim a woman's "fundamental right" to abortion. They insist with moral conviction that "love makes a family." They condemn "Bush's immoral war in Iraq." The question, then, is not whether there are truths about such things as the morality of abortion and the nature of marriage; the question in each case is: What is the truth?

The central and decisive truth about human embryos and fetuses is that they are living individuals of the species *Homo sapiens*—members of the human family—at early stages of their natural development. Each of us was once an embryo, just as each of us was once an adolescent, a child, an infant, and a fetus. Each of us developed from the embryonic into and through the fetal, infant, child, and adolescent stages of our lives, and into adulthood, with his or her distinctness, unity, and identity fully intact. We were never mere "parts" of our mothers; we were, from the beginning, complete, self-integrating organisms that developed to maturity by a gradual, gapless, and self-directed process.

Our foundational principle of the profound, inherent, and equal dignity of every human being demands that all members of the human family be respected and protected irrespective not merely of race, sex, and ethnicity, but also of age, size, location, stage of development, and condition of dependency. Even if we were to adopt a strict libertarian position on the role of government, the facts of human embryology and developmental biology, combined with the commitment—shared by conservatives of all stripes, including libertarians—to honoring the dignity of each human individual, would compel us to strive to protect, through the law, the child in the womb as well as the embryonic human being who happens to begin his existence in a petri dish. Notice that it would not be enough merely to look for ways to cut the abortion rate and to search for ethical means of obtaining stem cells of the type procured today by killing human embryos. These are worthy goals, to be sure, but justice demands more. It demands the protection of the law. To exclude anyone from the law's protection is to treat him unjustly.

Of course, politics is the art of the possible. And, as Frederick Douglass reminded us in his tribute to Lincoln after the president's assassination, public opinion (and other constraints) sometimes limits what can be done at the moment to advance any just cause. The pro-life movement has in recent years settled on an incrementalist strategy for protecting nascent human life. So long as incrementalism is not a euphemism for surrender or neglect or compromises that leave grave injustices permanently in place, it can be entirely honorable. The goal must be to accomplish in law and policy all that can be accomplished in the prevailing circumstances, while working to move public opinion in directions more respectful of human life so as to make possible further advances in law and policy. Indeed, often it is the small victories in the political domain that help get public opinion moving in the right direction, thus establishing the conditions for greater achievements. Planting premises in the law whose logic demands, in the end, full respect for all members of the human family can be a valuable thing to do, even where those premises seem modest.

Two recent achievements of the pro-life movement offer examples of this way of proceeding. The first is Professor Arkes's Born-Alive Infants Protection Act, passed by Congress when it was in Republican hands and signed into law by President Bush. By formally protecting the handful of children each year who survive abortions despite the abortionists' best efforts to dispatch them, the act plants in the law the proposition that the developing child is a being whose claims on us do not depend on whether someone else happens to want him or her. The act pressed upon supporters of abortion a profoundly uncomfortable question: Is the right to abortion a right to be free of pregnancy or a right to destroy a developing child? If the latter—and, of course, destroying the child is the abortionist's precise objective—then what is the moral or logical argument against supporting the exercise of the right once the child has been delivered from its mother's body? Why isn't the right to abortion the right to an *effective* abortion? Yet even most supporters of abortion recoil at the thought of killing the child outside the womb—even if he or she has been targeted for abortion. Marxist professors used to describe strategies of this sort as "heightening the contradictions." If people are opposed to killing the child when she is "out," how can they find it acceptable to kill her when she happens to be "in"? She is, after all, the same child.

The other great recent legislative accomplishment of the pro-life movement was getting a ban on partial-birth abortions through Congress and onto the desk of a president who was willing to sign it. The debate over partial-birth abortion has been extremely helpful in focusing the public's attention on what abortion is. It has deeply damaged the efforts of the pro-abortion movement to cover up the reality of abortion with euphemisms such as "termination of pregnancy," "products of conception," and "choice." It has brought certain facts home to many Americans who were perhaps a bit unsure of them: "It's a child, not a choice"; "Abortion stops a beating heart"; "A fetus is not potential life, but a life with potential." These are slogans, to be sure, but they have the very considerable advantage of being true.

At the same time, sonography is reinforcing the message. Improvements in this technology offer a virtual window into the womb. There we view the wondrous and wondrously human life of the child before he or she is born. Among the goals that the pro-life movement should continue to pursue with vigor is making high-quality sonography more widely available. Predictably—and understandably—the forces of abortion are fighting this, even claiming that sonograms should be avoided because they may harm the fetus! Public resources as well as private funds can help here, especially when it comes to supporting the compassionate, woman-affirming work of pro-life clinics around the country.

Speaking of these clinics, we should be promoting candidates for legislative office who will, in federal and state chambers, have the courage and strength to work for the defunding of abortion promoters at home and abroad, and the funding of those who aid pregnant women in need by offering them moral and material support, protection from abusive boyfriends or others, adoption services, and other forms of assistance. The pro-life movement is genuinely pro-mother and pro-child, though the abortion-supporting media rarely give it credit for this. The using of taxpayer dollars to promote deliberate feticide is a grave abuse of governmental power and contradicts the most fundamental moral purpose of government: the protection of innocent life. By contrast, and contrary to an extreme libertarian view of the moral limits of governmental power, the use of governmental resources to combat a gravely unjust practice such as abortion, by for example supporting private organizations (whether faith-based or not), is consistent with a sound understanding of the scope of governmental power to protect basic rights and advance the common good.

Abortion is an issue of profound moral significance. Our posture toward it determines to a large extent whether we truly are what we aspire to be: a people "dedicated to the proposition" that all are created equal. But a specter yet graver than abortion haunts us as biotechnology moves forward. Now, there is much in biotechnology to applaud. Various technologies will bring healing and relieve human suffering without raising moral concerns. No one should be "against" biotechnology. It is a good thing, indeed a very good thing, and government should encourage and support it *to the extent that it respects basic moral principles, especially the sanctity of human life.*

Fully just law would protect all innocent human life. Yet sometimes this is not, or not yet, possible in the concrete political circumstances of the moment. Today, for example, we do not have the political strength to protect "spare" human embryos in cryopreservation units that can under prevailing law be destroyed, or donated for research in which they are destroyed to obtain stem cells. By wielding his veto pen, President Bush has blocked any federal funding for research that involves killing human embryos or using embryos whose destruction would be encouraged if federal funding for research in which they are used were available. And that is a significant pro-life achievement. Yet privately funded embryo-destructive research remains lawful.

Interestingly, however, most parents of cryopreserved embryos are unwilling to destroy them or donate them for research, though some see donating them to science as a way to do something beneficial with them once the decision has been made not to use them for another pregnancy. The pro-life movement rightly rejected the argument that research in which these embryos are destroyed is morally acceptable, and should be eligible for federal funding, because "the embryos are going to die anyway." Just as we recoil from harvesting organs even from death-row inmates who "are going to die anyway," we should not permit human beings in any stage or condition to be reduced to disposable research material.

The real issue, though, is not the use of cryopreserved embryos produced by *in vitro* fertilization. This is merely a stalking horse. The real issue is the practice of creating human embryos by cloning to be destroyed either in the blastocyst stage (days five to six) or later in gestation. I say this for two reasons. First, there are not nearly enough cryopreserved embryos for use in the research scientists wish to do. If, in fact, embryonic stem cells become usable in therapies to treat major diseases—indeed, even if they prove useful in treating a single major disease—hundreds of thousands of embryos, perhaps millions, will be needed in relatively short order. Second, *in vitro* embryos are all products of the genetic lottery. They are not a genetic match to the patient who would be treated. As with vital organ transplantation, this raises the likelihood of rejection and the need for immunosuppression and other medical interventions that create difficulties and dangers of their own. Cloning holds out the possibility of providing a magic bullet to solve the problem. Since the embryonic clone would be a twin of the donor, the rejection problem would probably be very substantially reduced. Cloning has not yet been perfected, but it very likely will be. Thus we face the prospect of human life being manufactured on a massive scale in order to be destroyed in biomedical work.

Stem cells of the sort we now have debates about—those obtained by destroying human embryos in the blastocyst stage—cannot currently be used in therapies and may never prove to be therapeutically useful. Despite the promises of magic cures, these stem cells—whether obtained from *in vitro* embryos or (judging from nonhuman animal experimentation) clones—are highly unstable and tend to generate tumors. That is why there is not a single embryonic-stem-cell therapy even in stage one of clinical trials. (By contrast, there are a large number of trials in progress using nonembryonic cells, such as those obtained harmlessly from umbilical-cord blood, bone marrow, and other uncontroversial sources.) Apparently, no one quite knows even how to begin thinking about the extraordinarily complex challenges of stabilizing embryonic cells so that they can be used in therapies.

No one, that is, except Mother Nature. And this raises another alarming prospect—and a moral challenge to be met. As the embryo develops *in utero*, its cells are stabilized by a remarkable process of intercellular communication. After several weeks or a few months, they in effect stabilize each other while retaining their pluripotency—that is, their capacity to be transformed into various forms of tissue. Experiments with cows show that the problem of tumor formation can be overcome by cloning embryos, implanting them, allowing them to gestate to a certain developmental point, then aborting the developing calves, and harvesting stem cells from them. When these cells are then injected into the cows from which the cloned fetal calves were created, there is no evidence of tumor formation. Do you see where this goes?

Legislation in several states, including my home state of New Jersey, proposes to make state funding available for the macabre practice of human fetal farming. It is difficult to imagine a more egregious abuse of governmental power. Congress, however, was persuaded to pass a preemptive ban on the practice, which President Bush signed. This is a fine example of the pro-life movement's looking ahead to problems likely to arise three to five years down the road and acting while public opinion is favorable. Most Americans are horrified by the idea of creating a human life, gestating it, and aborting it to harvest cells and tissues. Even most supporters of abortion are repulsed by this possibility—at least for now. But for those who would like to go down that path, there is always hope that the promise of miracle cures can be used to erode public resistance. Hence the legislation in New Jersey and elsewhere, laying the groundwork for fetal farming. Although the congressional prohibition is an important achievement, it includes a loophole that should be closed: technically, it would not be illegal to gestate an embryo in an *artificial* womb. This perhaps sounds outlandish, but such technologies might well become available in the not-too-distant future. With that possibility in view, we should press Congress to return to the issue.

Our long-term goal should be a comprehensive ban on all forms of human cloning, including the creation of embryos to be destroyed in research. Senator Sam Brownback has led the fight for this in the U.S. Senate, and he deserves hearty congratulations for his leadership. Unfortunately, several Senate seats will have to be taken from pro-cloning members if a cloning ban is to be achieved. Legal cloning would be bad enough, but the pro-cloning forces in Congress have a long-term goal of their own: federal funding for the creation of re-search embryos by cloning. If there is a true moral nightmare in our future, it is a massive, federally funded industry in the manufacture and destruction of human beings.

Let me now turn to the issue of marriage. The institution of mar-riage is battered in our culture, but it is not lost. Private pro-marriage forces, such as Marriage Savers, are doing important work through churches and other institutions. Much damage to the critically im-portant marriage culture was done by bad legislation and policy, al-most always in the name of reform. That legislation and policy is now itself in need of reform.

If we are to restore and secure the institution of marriage, we must recover a sound understanding of what marriage is and why it is in the public interest for law and policy to take cognizance of it and support it. Marriage is a prepolitical form of association—what might be called a natural institution. It is not created by law, though law recognizes and regulates it in every culture. Nowhere is it treated as a purely private matter, the way we (rightly) treat baptisms and bar mitzvahs. Some on the libertarian fringe toy with the idea that mar-riage could in fact be privatized, and even some who are not on the fringe wonder whether that might be the best solution to the contro-versy over same-sex "marriage."

I understand why someone would consider this idea, but it strikes me as a very bad one. There is a reason that all cultures treat marriage as a matter of public concern and even recognize it in law and regu-late it. The family is the fundamental unit of society. It is the original and best department of health, education, and welfare. Governments rely on families to produce something that governments on their own could not possibly produce—namely, upright, decent people who make honest, law-abiding, public-spirited citizens. And marriage is the indispensable foundation of the family. Although all marriages in all cultures have their imperfections, children flourish in an environ-ment where they benefit from the love and care of both mother and father, and from the committed and exclusive love of their parents for each other.

Anyone who believes in limited government should firmly reject the privatization of marriage and strongly back government support for it. Does this sound paradoxical? The apparent paradox is easily dissolved. In the absence of a strong marriage culture, families fail to form; when they do form they are often unstable; absentee fathers become a serious problem; out-of-wedlock births are common; and a train of social pathologies follows. With families failing to perform their health, education, and welfare functions, the demand for government to step in grows, whether in the form of greater policing or as a provider of other social services. Bureaucracies must be created, and they inexorably expand—indeed they become powerful lobbyists for their own preservation and expansion. Everyone suffers—with the poorest and most vulnerable (and therefore most reliant on a healthy marriage culture) suffering most. Someone has to pay for policing and massively increased social services, and that someone is of course the taxpayer. Anyone who cares about the plight of the poor, and anyone who believes the government takes too much of the people's money, should think about the role marriage plays in a healthy society and join the effort to revitalize and protect it.

I have in other writings made the moral case for the conjugal conception of marriage as the union of one man and one woman pledged to permanence and fidelity and committed to caring for children who come as the fruit of their matrimonial union. I have argued that acceptance of the idea that two persons of the same sex could actually be married to each other would make nonsense of key features of marriage, and would necessarily require abandoning any ground of principle for supposing that marriage is the union of only two persons, as opposed to three or more. Only a thin veneer of sentiment, if it happens to exist, can prevent acceptance of polyamory as a legitimate marital option once we have given up the principle of marriage as a male-female union. To those arguments, I will here add an additional reason to reject the very idea of same-sex "marriage": namely, that the acceptance of the idea would result in a massive undermining of religious liberty and family autonomy as supporters of same-sex "marriage" would, in the name of equality, demand the use of governmental power to whip into line those institutions of civil society who continued to honor their own conscientious commitment to the conjugal conception of marriage. The experience of Massachusetts as well as foreign jurisdictions is that once marriage is compromised or formally redefined, principles of nondiscrimination are quickly used as cudgels against religious communities and families who wish to uphold by precept and example true marriage.

The effective defense of marriage against the current onslaught will require an understanding of what marriage is (and is not) as a matter of moral truth. Practical or pragmatic arguments are, as I said earlier, legitimate and important. But too few pro-marriage politicians are willing to say much about what marriage actually is, perhaps because their understanding of it, though perfectly sound, is informal and implicit. This gives those who would abolish the conjugal conception of marriage an important advantage in public debate. They hammer away with their rhetoric of "love makes a family" and demand to know how anyone's marriage would be threatened if the same-sex partners next door were also allowed to "marry." (Of course, if love makes a family, then seven people who love each other and wish to express that love in a sexual partnership can be married to each other, and presumably their "marriage" would no more harm their neighbors' marriages than would the "marriage" of a same-sex couple.)

Part of the trouble pro-marriage politicians and others have in defending marriage against the pathologies afflicting it follows from the fact that these pathologies are widespread, and supporters of marriage, being human, are not immune to them. This is not to excuse anyone from personal responsibility. But the fact is that sustaining a marriage despite the collapse of many of its social supports is difficult for anyone. In trying to stand up for marriage, political leaders, intellectuals, and activists who have had marital problems of their own are subjected to charges of hypocrisy. Many therefore censor themselves. As a result, the pro-marriage movement loses the leadership of some of its most talented people.

The question of same-sex "marriage" is critically important, but rebuilding and renewing the marriage culture goes far beyond it. By abolishing the basic understanding of marriage as an inherently conjugal union, legal recognition of same-sex "marriage" would be disastrous. But many would say that such recognition would simply ratify the collapse of marriage that followed from widespread divorce, non-marital sexual cohabitation, and other factors having nothing to do with homosexual conduct. It is certainly true that the origins of the pathologies afflicting marriage lie in such factors. Rebuilding the marriage culture will require careful, incremental legal reforms to, for example, roll back unilateral divorce, accompanied by Herculean efforts on the part of nongovernmental institutions—especially churches and other religious bodies—to prepare couples more adequately for marriage, help them establish and nurture strong marital relationships, and assist those who are dealing with marital problems. Public-private partnerships will be essential, in my view, to cutting the divorce rate and locking in the cuts. This won't be easy. If marriage weren't so important, it wouldn't be worth trying.

As with abortion, same-sex "marriage" is being advanced by liberal activist judges who exercise creative powers of constitutional interpretation. That gives us reason to pursue with new dedication the larger fight against the judicial usurpation of democratic legislative authority—another profound abuse of governmental power. State courts have given the supporters of same-sex marriage some important early victories, especially in Massachusetts, Vermont, and New Jersey (though in the latter two states the courts did not order that the word "marriage" be attached to legally recognized same-sex partnerships), and those supporters are in a position to fight hard to secure their gains in democratic forums and even to advance them.

Despite extraordinarily broad support for same-sex "marriage" among elites (including, of course, the universities and the media), initiatives to preserve marriage as the union of one man and one woman have prevailed, usually by decisive margins, every time they have been put on the ballot but once. (The sole exception—Arizona—already had a legal definition of marriage as a male-female union in its state law, and there were other unusual complications.) Even in the blue state of Wisconsin, a marriage initiative prevailed in a near-landslide last November—in the course of what was around the country a big night for Democrats. With the Federal Marriage Amendment stalled—even many Republicans unwisely declining to support it—state marriage initiatives and constitutional amendments are vitally important. The issue should be taken to the people at every possible opportunity. Even in the bluest states, marriage will have a stronger chance with the people than with the judges. Indeed, marriage fares better with the people than with their elected representatives. The California state legislature passed a same-sex "marriage" bill. Governor Arnold Schwarzenegger, though hardly a great defender of conjugal marriage, vetoed the bill because it contradicted a recent referendum in which a proposition defining marriage as the union of a man and a woman passed by a large margin.

I suspect that all of the Republican candidates for president this year—and possibly all of the Democratic candidates—will say they oppose same-sex marriage and favor retaining the definition of marriage as the union of a man and a woman. Every one of them should be asked this question: Why?

If they don't know why they believe that marriage is a conjugal union, or can't say, then they are unlikely to be much help—or even to be willing to expend much effort—in preserving it.

The next question each candidate should be asked is: What are you going to do to ensure that marriage remains the union of a man and a woman? And they should not be let off the hook easily. Some will give an answer about federalism, and supporters of marriage will have to decide whether they find this answer adequate. I do not. Just as the nation could not endure half-slave and half-free but eventually had to go one way or the other, we will not be able to get by with a situation in which some couples are "married" in one state, not married when they move to or travel through the next, and married again when they reach a third. If same-sex "marriage" is legally recognized in a small number of states, it will spread throughout the nation, either through judicial action under the Constitution's Full Faith and Credit Clause or by virtue of informal cultural pressures. Some states may try to hold out, but the courts will eventually force them into line. That is why we need a national resolution of the issue, and probably a constitutional one. Believers in marriage did not start this fight, and we are loath to interfere with traditional state powers—precisely because we view federalism as serving limited government and embodying our belief in the principle of subsidiarity. But judicial usurpation has put into operation a chain of events that will result in the radical redefinition of marriage unless action is taken at the national level—going beyond the Defense of Marriage Act (which may yet be struck down by the courts)—to preserve the conjugal conception of marriage. That is why I will want to know from candidates seeking my vote whether they are prepared to support the Federal Marriage Amendment. We are still a long way from having the votes in Congress to pass it, but that is all the more reason to demand leadership from conservative politicians.

Finally, there is the question of civil unions. Some candidates will say they are against same-sex unions but in favor of legal recognition of same-sex partnerships, with all or most of the rights and responsibilities of marriage, only falling under a different rubric. If law and policy are at least to do no harm to marriage, it is critical that they avoid treating nonmarital conduct and relationships as if they were marital. There are clear moral lines—and not merely semantic ones—between what is marital and what is not, and the law should respect them. If they are blurred or erased, the public understanding of the meaning of marriage will erode.

Some of the benefits traditionally associated with marriage may legitimately be made more widely available in an effort to meet the needs of people who are financially interdependent with a person or persons to whom they are not married. Private contracts between such people should be sufficient to accomplish most of what they consider desirable. If, however, a jurisdiction moves in the direction of creating a formalized system of domestic partnerships, it is critical that the privileges, immunities, and other benefits and responsibilities contained in the package offered to nonmarried partners *not* be predicated on the existence or presumption of a sexual relationship between them. Benefits should be made available to, for example, a grandparent and adult grandchild who are living together and caring for each other. The needs that domestic-partnership schemes seek to address have nothing to do with whether the partners share a bed and what they do in it. The law should simply take no cognizance of the question of a sexual relationship. It should not, that is, treat a nonmarital sexual relationship as a public good.

The defense of life against abortion and cloning calls America back to the founding principles of our regime and to reflection on the justifying point and purposes of law and government. The defense of marriage, meanwhile, shores up the cultural preconditions for a regime of democratic republican government dedicated to human equality, fundamental human rights, and principled limits on state powers. These causes are therefore not to be considered as a distraction from other pressing goals, such as economic growth, environmental protection, and the defense of the nation against terrorism. They are, rather, causes that spring from the foundational moral purposes of law and the state.

six

Daniel N. Robinson

"RIGHTS" AND OUR ESSENTIAL NATURE

My aim in this chapter is to highlight rather than resolve a conflict that arises from a noble sentiment and worthy moral precept. As
persons and as nations, the civilized world has developed a still enlarging respect for the dignity of the individual and for the value that
persons attach to their cultures and countries. As persons and as nations, the civilized world is reminded daily of practices judged to be
barbaric and irrational, but nonetheless thoroughly integrated into
the lives and beliefs of those who engage in them.

Examples are not hard to find. Especially controversial is female
genital mutilation, common in certain Muslim communities for some
fourteen centuries and, on some accounts, permitted if not required
by one or another passage in the Koran. The Sunnah of the Prophet
makes reference to the practice and comments only on the need for

care in bringing about the desired result.[1] China, even as we meet, officially conducts programs of organ removal from the living to meet the ever enlarging international demand. We can be sure the Chinese authorities would not claim immunity on religious grounds but surely would warn others not to interfere with "domestic policy." There is broad support within today's intellectual communities that such warnings are valid and are to be heeded, "Who are we," goes the insistent question, "to tell *them* how to live?" Just as preserving or ending the lives of fetuses is, as they say, a personal and private decision—just as the life of Terry Schiavo was none of the government's business—so the mutilation of the genital organs of young girls or the extraction of organs from the living must have the benefit of noninterference.

There is a political dimension to all this, of course, typically sketched in terms of "pluralism" and the need to make peace with many others who do not share what we are pleased to call "our values." I might pause here to note that this, too, inclines us toward paradox, for there is something entirely paradoxical in requiring an unblinking tolerance toward others. The paradox is that the beneficiaries sooner or later will include those who will, on the occasion of their victory, put an end to all tolerance. This is a related but different issue from that which I address today. Returning to that issue, I ask, what are we to make of "pluralism" and its alleged authority? For this, I turn to Montesquieu's *Persian Letters*.[2]

The *Persian Letters* and Pluralism

The *Persian Letters* were published in 1721 and illustrate the literary adroitness and keen understanding that fashioned Montesquieu

1. See on this point Nawal El-Saadawi, *The Hidden Face of Eve: Women in the Arab World,* trans. Sherif Hetata. (New York: Zed Press, 1980), 33. Other sources raise doubts about this interpretation. But the practice goes on.

2. Montesquieu, *Persian Letters,* trans. C. J. Betts (Harmondsworth, U.K.: Penguin Books, 1973). (Original work published 1721.)

very much the man for his season, which was the Enlightenment. In this satirical work comprised of 161 letters exchanged between two Persian brothers, Montesquieu illustrates two aspects of Enlightenment thought easily misunderstood as incompatible. There is first the appreciation of the wide diversity of cultural values adopted by human communities, a diversity so great as to render some societies nearly unintelligible to others. But then there is the equally developed recognition of the point at which diversity is so inimical to the enduring interests of human communities as to threaten their very survival. We see this with painful clarity in Usbek's account of the Troglodytes in *Letter 11*.

In *Letter 11* in which Usbek relates the tale of the Troglodytes by way of replying to his friend Mirza's question regarding the right sort of life to live. Mirza wonders whether virtue or sensual pleasure should be the goal, and Usbek answers by rehearsing the fate of the Troglodytes—savage, "more like animals than men.... so wicked and ferocious that there were no principles of equity or justice among them." They murder their leaders, reject all authority, and commit themselves—each one singly—to pursue one's own interests, indifferent to the needs and desires of anyone else. Each Troglodyte grows just so much food as he needs, provides for his own defense, and practices the arts of self-gratification. It is not long, however, before crop failures in one area, then in another, as well as unevenly distributed misfortunes lead to the death of many. On top of this, there were still other grave consequences. Thus,

> One of the leading citizens had a very beautiful wife. His neighbour fell in love with her and abducted her. This caused a great quarrel, and after a good deal of insults and fighting they agreed to abide by the decision of a Troglodyte who, while the Republic had lasted, had had a certain amount of influence. They went to him, wanting to present their arguments. "What does it matter to me," he said, "if this woman belongs to you, or to you? I have my land to plough; I am certainly not going to spend my time patching up your disputes, and looking after

your affairs while I neglect my own. Please leave me in peace, and don't trouble me any more with your quarrels."

Finally, with the outbreak of a virulent disease, the Troglodytes searched out a doctor who had come from the nearby land, imploring him to provide remedies, which he did, only to discover that his patients had no intention of paying him. The epidemic returned but this time the doctor refused all treatment, informing the Troglodytes,

> You are unjust. In your souls is a poison deadlier than that for which you want a cure. You do not deserve to have a place on earth, because you have no humanity, and the rules of equity are unknown to you. It seems to me that I should be offending against the gods, who are punishing you, if I were to oppose their rightful anger.

Well, what about the Troglodytes? Maybe they just "evolved" that way. One pervasive influence arising from the Darwinian revolution is skepticism toward or outright rejection of notions of enduring and immutable properties within the biosocial sphere. Even the progressive philosophies of the eighteenth-century Enlightenment, and Montesquieu is exemplary here, though granting the protean nature of human nature, assumed all along that favoring conditions would permit the realization of authentic lives, the distinctly human life available to all who were liberated from superstition, ignorance, and tyranny. The famous voyages of that century, especially those of Captain Cook, did not result in relativistic anthropologies but in an ever more confident conviction that the engines of political and scientific progress would soon bring light and hope to the world's undeveloped cultures.[3]

In a word, the Enlightenment project was not deterred but challenged by the Troglodyte, for the project was grounded in an essentialist anthropology. It was not in the ambit of that project to reach the possibility that "human nature," in contrast with human "personality," was unstable, episodic, and subject to alteration at the most

3. James Cook, *Captain Cook's Journal during the First Voyage Round the World* (London: Elliot Stock, 1893), available online at http://www.gutenberg.org/etext/8106.

fundamental level. Rather, one's "personal identity" was a matter of experiential and contextual determinants, but one's essential identity was the abiding ground.

Largely as a result of evolutionary principles, this perspective has changed, replaced or seriously challenged by one of instability, probability, organicity. One cannot identify, let alone "legislate," a set of core precepts applicable to humanity wherever it is found. Rather, pluralism is not merely a social fact but an evolutionary inevitability as human communities come to their own terms with environmental pressures. The tension is less between pleasure and virtue than between a realistic conception of "virtue" as nothing more than what a given culture, under its own defining pressures, values in the makeup of its members. Yet, against all of this is the comparably "official" view that there must be "international courts of justice" to protect the cause of "human rights" according to principles taken to be universal. There seems to be a problem here…

The Ship of Theseus: Locke and Personal Identity

In the life of Theseus, Plutarch cites unnamed ancient philosophers vexed by an aspect of the Theseus myth. Considering the old planks replaced by new wood on the ship Theseus had sailed to Crete, they wondered at what point the refurbished ship was no longer "the ship of Theseus." Plutarch writes of it thus:

> The ship wherein Theseus and the youth of Athens returned had thirty oars, and was preserved by the Athenians down even to the time of Demetrius Phalereus, for they took away the old planks as they decayed, putting in new and stronger timber in their place, insomuch that this ship became a standing example among the philosophers, for the logical question as to things that grow; one side holding that the ship remained the same, and the other contending that it was not the same.[4]

4. This translation can be accessed via http://classics.mit.edu/Plutarch/theseus.html.

The problem, as modern as it is ancient, is that of the continuity of identity for anything that undergoes change; the problem of when the "essence" of a thing no longer obtains, such that the thing is no longer the sort of thing it was. How can it be said, for example, that between conception and death at an old age, the entity in question retains a continuing identity? For, to answer that nothing else ever occupied the space this entity occupied at any and every instant of time, would merely establish a continuity of mass or volume, and surely not a continuity of identity.

Among the several legacies of so-called Aristotelianism that the modern age of science took to be counterfeit, the very concept of essence—*ousia*—was subjected to sustained criticism. This is a long and interesting chapter in the history of ideas but one beyond the purposes of this chapter. It is sufficient to pick up the account with Locke's well-known distinction between what he called the real essence of a thing and its nominal essence, and then briefly consider the distinction in the context of personal identity.

Locke develops the distinction between "real" and "nominal" essences in book 3, chapter 6 of *An Essay Concerning Human Understanding.*[5] Here he notes that any number of creatures of his general form, or of considerably different form, might have more or better faculties than he, but that such differences are not in any way "essential to the one or the other, or to any individual whatever, till the mind refers it to some sort or species of things." What will give Locke or anyone else that continuing identity that might have been incorrectly regarded as one's "real essence" is no more than that on which the various habits and dispositions of the mind settle. Thus, man is essentially (1) a rational being, (2) a social being, and (3) a being able to report dreams, etc.

Locke gave the problem of personal identity its modern formulation. One of the aims of his *Essay Concerning the Human Under-*

5. John Locke, *An Essay Concerning Human Understanding,* 2 vols., ed. A. C. Fraser (New York: Dover Press, 1959 [1690]), 1.460.

standing was precisely to challenge *essentialism*. Faithful to Newtonian science, Locke regarded the *real* essence of a thing to be beyond the powers of sense, grounded in its fundamental corpuscular structure, and manifesting itself, if at all, only at that perceptible level on which variable and context-dependent *nominal essences* are fashioned. Locke's *real* essence is a congeries of submicroscopic particles held together by gravitational forces, but perceived in ways that generate such *nominal* characterizations as "physician friend to the Earl of Shaftesbury," "Fellow of the Royal Society," and "a rational animal." These characterizations arise from conventional discourse, the contingencies of culture and context, and the nuances of perception, memory, and mental life. Extended by later and then by contemporary writers, this line of analysis culminates in the concept of a person as a social construct, a cultural artifact, whose "essential" nature is but a nominal essence, different from different points of view.

But there is another Locke. The Locke of the *Essay Concerning Human Understanding* is rather more "metaphysical" than the author of those *Two Treatises of Civil Government* that were among the most widely reprinted works of the eighteenth century. In this seminal political treatise, Locke looks less to Newton than to Stoic philosophy in arguing that,

> the Law of Nature stands as an Eternal Rule to all Men, Legislators as well as others. The Rules that they make for other Mens Actions, be conformable to the Law of Nature, i.e. to the Will of God, of which that is a Declaration, and the fundamental Law of Nature being the preservation of Mankind, no Humane Sanction can be good, or valid against it.[6]

To invoke a universal law of nature as dispositive in human affairs is to extend Newton's laws into regions vastly more cluttered and dynamic than celestial mechanics. Moreover, it is to assume something about human nature itself that goes beyond social conventions and cultural

---

6. John Locke, *Two Treatises of Government,* ed. Peter Laslett (Cambridge: Cambridge University Press, 1965), 358.

nuances. It is, indeed, to assume something essential about human nature, against which human sanctions themselves cannot safely or validly prevail.

What I hope to draw out from these few lessons from Locke is a measure of the costs incurred when essentialism is either abandoned or is reduced to a species of nominal essence capable of supporting the more pernicious forms of moral and juridical relativism. Still, the seasonal hibernation of essentialism is based on cogent criticisms warranting at least a summary and, I hope, judicious appraisal.

What Is It to Be a Natural Kind of Thing?

To speak of something having an essential nature, at least as Aristotle would intend the adjective to be understood, is to speak of what it is to be a certain kind of thing. As Aristotle used the term, "essence" is conveyed by the phrase *to ti ein einai*—the "what it is to be" something. But the "something" falls under a universal category. Thus, a cat is an animal, and were there no such *taxa* as plants and animals, there could be no cats as such. This is not to be confused with Platonic notions of "true forms," thought to have ontological standing apart from their actual instantiations. Rather, Aristotle—the great natural scientist and relentless taxonomist—recognizes degrees of kinship as expressed in the form of similar appearance, similar modes of behavior, similar responses to the environment. Thus, the sense in which "Coriscus is a man" is different from the sense in which "Coriscus is musical." Coriscus is *essentially* an instance of "what it is to be" a human being, but merely accidentally musical, along the way. As for the *to ti ein einai* of human beings, it is finally to be a rational animal, disposed naturally to social and political modes of life and able to base actions and choices on rational deliberation,

The *to ti ein einai* for this kind of creature includes centrally *fitness for the rule of law.* It is to be a specific "kind" of creature, arising from the natural order of things, as does the *polis* itself. To be "essentially" a something is to be so by nature, as in the pathetic example of the *doulos phusikos,* the "slave by nature." It is to be a *natural kind* of thing. But just how stable are those general classes taken to be "natural kinds"? Alexander Bird gives a hint as to the complexity of the problem:

> When one visits a greengrocer, in the section devoted to fruit one will find, among other things, apples, strawberries, blackcurrants, rhubarb, and plums, while the vegetable display will present one with potatoes, cabbages, carrots, tomatoes, peppers and peas. If one were to ask a botanist to classify these items we will find rhubarb removed from the list of fruit and tomatoes and peppers added.... Following this line ... one might conclude that there really is no absolute sense in which there is a natural classification of things into kinds.[7]

I cite this to underscore the difficulties with notions of "natural kinds," but these are not fatal to the concept metaphysically and cause it no embarrassment whatever practically. After all, a rose by any other name would smell as sweet.

"Essentializing" as a Cognitive Function

We have persistent reminders that reality and our cognitive access to it are not finally reducible to culture and context, and almost certainly not confined to the realm of changeable observable properties. Nor is it telling against essentialism that it arises from a set of cognitive dispositions widely shared across time and cultures. If, indeed, there is a nearly ubiquitous disposition not only to describe or understand nature in essentialist terms, and if this disposition has proven to be a necessary feature of adjusting to the physical affordances of nature, then the burden would shift to the antiessentialist. At the end of the day, the pragmatic dimension of cognition is decisive, though arguments will abound as to how close we are to the end of the day, and as to what the measure of efficacy is to be.

It is worth noting in this connection that, whether or not there

7. Alexander Bird, *Philosophy of Science* (London: UCL Press, 1998), 96–97.

are real essences and fixed natural kinds, both children and adults habitually perceive and organize aspects of the external world in essentialist fashion. There is a substantial literature addressed to what has been called "psychological essentialism" based largely on evolutionary principles that would establish the adaptive advantage gained by this mode of cognition. The processes at work are not of the descriptive empirical sort: What one regards as the "essence" of a thing is not exhausted by its observable features alone but arises from a conception of some internal, intrinsic feature that causally brings about these features.[8] Having established the "essence" of the thing, an observer is able to anticipate any number of actions and features not now or yet observed, but readily inducible from, alas, the "essence" of the thing.

Yet another adaptive feature of psychological essentialism is that it disposes the percipient to classify objects according to potential effects even while remaining ignorant of that "executive cause" by which the effects are brought about. An example is that of food types that are poisonous (e.g., mushrooms), animal kinds that are "predatory," etc. The adaptive advantage gained by this mode of cognition is obvious. In all, and though I am notoriously impatient with "sociobiological" explanations of complex phenomena, I cite these findings to make clear that the "essentializing" disposition is not some relic of an age of superstition and ignorance, but a constant support on which success in the routine affairs of life depends. Where the arguments of the metaphysicians come down more or less equally on the various sides of a question, the pragmatist need not be so humble as to withhold his own validating criteria. And, to the extent that data of any sort might be admissible even within the often antiseptic arena of metaphysical speculation, it would seem that the record of human social and political organization might be adduced in support of the

8. A recent review of the literature has been provided by H. Clark Barrett, "On the Functional Origins of Essentialism," *Mind and Society* 2, no. 3 (2001): 1–30. For a recent book on essentialism in cognitive development, see Susan Gelman, *The Essential Child: Origins of Essentialism in Everyday Thought* (New York: Oxford University Press, 2003).

proposition that, exceptions duly noted and explained, "man" seems very much and essentially to be a rational creature disposed to live in the company of others and to ground the patterns of social interaction in principles of a recognizably moral nature.

Owing to this same and irreducibly essentialist conception of human nature, they are able to predict a wide range of actions under virtually limitless conditions that might at some point be faced by us and those like us.

Fitness for the Rule of Law

To refer to an irreducibly *essentialist* conception may be confusing if not qualified by the sense of "essential" intended here. Lest the argument be misunderstood as a textbook example of the Naturalistic Fallacy, I emphasize that psychological research on the cognitive dispositions of children and adults will not and cannot settle or even address the metaphysical question pertaining to essences and natural kinds. Logicians and metaphysicians have struggled with *essentia* for more than two millennia, their efforts resisting tidy summary. As it it is to be understood here, the thesis of essentialism takes the "stereotype" *fit for the rule of law* as embracing entities possessed of specific powers. These may well be dependent to some extent on the right sort of brain, etc., but nothing of a biological or physical nature is sufficient to explain these powers. To make the point in another way, the essentialism that grounds "fitness for the rule of law" as I intend this to be understood here, is tied to the pragmatic functions of discourse, especially within the domains of law and morality. Any number of questions can be nontendentiously raised about the threshold of rationality below which an entity fails to qualify for life under the rule of law; but, again, the history of actual practices, recovered from widely different cultures and contexts, is surprisingly unambiguous in identifying those features that do render an entity fit for the rule of law, its protections, and its punishments.

For economy of definition, I take "the rule of law" to be the institutional means by which rights and duties are publicized and are implemented in such a way as to secure ends conformable to the concept of law itself. Debates between latter-day legal positivists and latter-day natural law theorists remain lively and informing, but can be largely neglected here. Whether one sides with the Thomistic concept of law as "an ordinance of reason" promulgated by one responsible for the good of the community, or with Austin, for whom law was no more than a command issued by an authority capable of coercive force, there remain incontestable presuppositions on which any rule of law must be based. Minimally, these include various powers and vulnerabilities attaching to those who would be thus ruled, as well as the capacity to act or to forebear from acting as a result of having at least minimal agentic power.

At this point, it is timely to consider the worrisome implications of theories of persons that treat moral and juridical canons as the artifacts of a given culture, their "cash value" amounting to little beyond local boundaries. If, as critics of essentialism would be likely to insist, the moral resources of a community arise from pragmatic challenges that are utterly contextual, there is no basis on which to regard the actual content of these moral resources as in any way absolute. The bones of frogs may have great value on that exotic island in the Pacific, but will not secure so much as a coffee and donut at *Starbucks*. Does this exhaust the nature of "rights" and of those fit to hold them? Do persons, as such, and in virtue of their now contested "essential" (or cognitively *essentialized*) attributes, bear *rights* that move with them, as it were, and if so, how far and to what degree?

A culture that claims a property interest in slaves would (as was clear in the famous U.S. case of *Dred Scott)* reject the claim that such an interest is terminated just in case the chattel is moved or moves itself to a jurisdiction that prohibits slavery. The latter jurisdiction might then refuse to return human chattel on the grounds that, at least in that jurisdiction, human beings cannot qualify as chattel property. What we are left with in such matters would seem to be little more than conflicting "values," these expressing nothing of an *essential* nature about reality. As the slaveholders leave their village and enter the cultural space of those who reject the very idea of slavery, they quickly discover that their "property rights" aren't moveable. Indeed, each village might claim on grounds of "village sovereignty" total immunity to the values and moral imperatives of neighbors. Rejected out of hand would be claims to the effect that in such matters neither national boundaries nor enduring local customs can vitiate the rights arising from the "essential" nature of the rights-bearer. Clearly, the position we are inclined to take in a matter of this sort will depend on what we take to be the nature and the ultimate grounding of "rights" as such. What are rights and on what basis may they be said to move with those that have them?

The concept of rights is different from concepts of privileges and licenses. A privilege—*privilegium*—entails the relaxation or suspension of a state of affairs, a law, or a requirement. A license is a form of permission granted on evidence of requisite competence or standing. Privileges and licenses are conferred and are revocable. What are taken to be—I will use the phrase without examining the range of options to which it is applied—what are taken to be *basic human rights* are precisely what no authority can revoke, for they are assumed to be possessed rather than given. But if this understanding is to rise higher than the level of a tautology, these "basic human rights" must be or must be grounded in what is indisputable at the level of ontology itself. The grounding must be something *real*.

I submit that "rights," thus understood, do match up with an essential rather than merely accidental or contingent aspects of being. Rights match up with the real *vulnerabilities* of beings capable of pain and suffering, capable of frustration and anguish, misery and loss. To paraphrase Aristotle, one might say that Coriscus does not have a *right* to be musical, though one might condemn a society that thwarted every honest effort Coriscus might expend in that direction. But if it is *essentially* the case that, for Coriscus as an adult to be a self-conscious, reflecting, motivated being, striving to create conditions of life consistent with the preservation and enhancement of these very essential features, then measures designed to suppress, thwart, or punish these very features are at the expense of Coriscus's *rights*. This is to say that *rights* as such are grounded in a class of vulnerabilities matching up with what enters into not merely the nominal essence of a human person but the actual psychophysical constitution of such a being.

Time does not permit a fuller examination of the specific rights arising from various classes of vulnerability. That examination was provided nearly a decade ago in an article I wrote with Rom Harre.[9] It is sufficient to note that not all vulnerabilities are avoidable; that many arise in ways independent of the actions of others; that some have little bearing on those interests that are properly secured by respect for rights. All too briefly, let me say that the vulnerabilities most clearly generative of rights are those that are subject to exploitation or enlargement at the hands of others, and are inextricably bound up with significant interests. Note, too, that an entity may *have* an interest without actually *taking* an interest. A child may *take* no interest in a will in which he has been named the principal beneficiary, but the child surely *has* an interest in it.

Moreover, to the extent that rights find their originating ontological niche in vulnerabilities, it is clear that they do not invariably require specific powers or capacities on the part of those for whom rights of one or another sort might be claimed. Thus, as creatures vulnerable to actions and events that cause severe pain, infants and puppies both can be said to have a right to be spared otherwise avoidable pain and suffering. It would be irrelevant to note, in such cases, that neither infants nor puppies had the power to claim such rights or even comprehend at a primitive level the concept of a right. Similarly, in virtue of those powers by which others can act and can bring

9. R. Harre and D. Robinson, "On the Primacy of Duties," *Philosophy* 70 (1995): 513–23.

about events, the possession of powers is what grounds *duties*. Again, it is entirely consistent to reserve rights to entities having no duties. The right of an infant to be spared painful treatment carries with it no duty on the part of the infant. Note, however, that some forms of pain or suffering or discomfort arise not from the essential nature of the creature, but from idiosyncratic desires, aspirations, and affections. Granting that Jack loves Jill and will be caused pain and suffering if rejected, it does not follow that Jack has a "right" to Jill's devotion. Rather, the vulnerabilities that ground rights are those properly classified as virtually universal in their distribution within the population of potential victims.

Clearly, at least on this understanding, rights match up with the essential properties of those entities for which rights are claimed. What is an essential property of one class of victims may occasion vulnerabilities not sustained in a different class. Adult persons within the social context are vulnerable to acts of libel. Infants within that same world are not. It would, therefore, be jejune to argue for an infant's "right" not to be libeled. Note, then, that even within a given species, the natural course of development itself results in the absence or the appearance of certain rights. Note also that actions intended to subvert natural development in order to prevent the appearance of just those vulnerabilities that would generate rights are themselves violations of rights.

It is by way of an irreducibly *essentialist* conception of human nature itself that the wrongfulness of the enlargement and exploitation of vulnerabilities is recognized as noncontextual, for our basic vulnerabilities are constitutive of our essential nature.

So, too, are those powers that render us fit for judgment. These powers at once are the occasion for duties and at the same time the source of unique vulnerabilities readily enlarged and exploited by regimes of law that are corrupt.

It now should be clear how rights move across national boundaries and otherwise test the confident antiessentialism of the moral relativist. National boundaries themselves are, needless to say, no more than the contingent and shifting facts of geopolitics and, as such, are not *essentially* anything. Accordingly, the fact that a given practice takes place here rather than there, or now rather than then, expresses nothing of an essential nature about the ontologically real features of the cosmos or sublunary places within it. But vulnerabilities and powers are ontologically real and defining, for they constitute the *to ti ein einai* of actual creatures and ground whatever one might coherently and consistently mean by a right and a duty. As these vulnerabilities and powers move with those in whom they are embodied, so too do the rights and duties. In this respect, it matters not a whit just where and when the movement takes place. Were it otherwise, there could be no crimes against humanity, no world court, no international human rights commission—in brief, none of the modern apparatus designed to protect the vulnerable, punish the offender, and otherwise record what a rational creature takes to be essential to a fully human form of life.

In the end, we may not be able to offer a detailed account of "human" and "humanity." As two of the leading investigators in this area of cognitive psychology have noted illustratively in relation to the concept of a bear,

> Essentialism does not entail that people know (consciously or unconsciously) what the essence is.... People may implicitly assume, for example, that there is some quality that bears share, that confers category identity and causes identifiable surface features, and they may use this belief to guide inductive inferences and explanations without being able to identify any feature or trait as the bear essence. This belief can be considered an unarticulated heuristic rather than a detailed theory.[10]

10. S. A. Gelman, and G. Diesendruck, "A Reconsideration of Concepts: On the Compatibility of Psychological Essentialism and Context Sensitivity," in *Conceptual Development: Piaget's Legacy,* ed. E. K. Scholnick, K. Nelson, S. A. Gelman, and P. H. Miller (Mahwah, N.J.: Lawrence Earlbaum, 1999), 88.

CONTRIBUTORS

Hadley Arkes is a senior fellow of the Ethics and Public Policy Center (EPPC) and a leading expert on American political philosophy, public policy, and constitutional law. His activities at EPPC include codirecting the program on the Constitution, the courts, and the culture. He is the Edward Ney Professor of Jurisprudence and American Institutions at Amherst College, where he has taught since 1966. He has written several books, including most recently *Natural Rights and the Right to Choose* (Cambridge University Press, 2002). His articles have appeared in numerous professional journals and media sources, including the *Wall Street Journal,* the *Washington Post,* the *Weekly Standard,* and the *National Review.* Professor Arkes was the main advocate, and architect of the bill that became known as the Born-Alive Infants Protection Act, which was signed into law in 2002. He has been the founder, at Amherst, of the Committee for the American Founding, a group of alumni and students seeking to preserve the doctrines of "natural rights" taught by the American Founders and Lincoln. Other recent books include *Gliding Serenely into Heresy* (2010) and *The Born Alive Act and the Undoing of Obama* (2008).

John M. Finnis is professor of law and legal philosophy at Oxford University, where he has held various positions since 1966. He has also been the Biolchini Family Professor of Law at the Notre Dame Law School since 1995. Professor Finnis has held positions at the University of California at Berkeley, Adelaide University, the University of Malawi, and Boston College. He teaches courses in jurisprudence; in the social, political, and legal theory of Thomas Aquinas; and in the social, political, and legal theory of Shakespeare. His service has included the Linacre Centre for Health Care Ethics, the Catholic Bishops' Joint Committee on Bioethical Issues, the International Theological Commission, the Pontifical Council for Justice and Peace, and the Pontifical Academy Pro Vita. He has published widely in law, legal theory, moral and political philosophy, moral theology, and the history of the late Elizabethan era. His most recent books are *Fundamentals of Ethics* (Georgetown University Press, 1983); *Nuclear Deterrence, Morality, and Realism* (Oxford University Press, 1988); *Moral Absolutes: Tradition, Revision, and Truth* (The Catholic University of America Press, 1991); *Aquinas: Moral, Political, and Legal Theory* (Oxford University Press, 1998); *The Collected Essays of John Finnis* (Oxford University Press, 2011); and the second edition of *Natural Law and Natural Rights* (Oxford University Press, 2011, orig. 1980).

Robert P. George is the McCormick Professor of Jurisprudence and director of the James Madison Program in American Ideals and Institutions at Princeton University. He is a member of the President's Council on Bioethics, and previously served as a presidential appointee to the United States Commission on Civil Rights and as a judicial fellow at the Supreme Court of the United States. Professor George has published numerous books and articles. His most recent books are *Embryo: A Defense of Human Life* (authored with Christopher Tollefsen; Doubleday, 2008); *Body-Self Dualism in Contemporary Ethics and Politics* (authored with Patrick Lee; Cambridge University Press, 2007); *The Meaning of Marriage* (edited with Jean Bethke Elshtain; Spence, 2006); *The Clash of Orthodoxies* (ISI Books, 2001); and *In Defense of Natural Law* (Oxford University Press, 2001). Among other awards, Professor George received a 2005 Bradley Prize for Intellectual and Civic Achievement. He holds honorary doctorates of law, letters, ethics, human letters, and science. In addition to his academic and civic work, he is Of Counsel to the law firm of Robinson & McElwee.

Livio Melina is vice-president (director) and professor of moral theology at the John Paul II Institute for Studies on Marriage and Family at the Lateran University in Rome. He holds a Ph.D. from the Universitá di Padova and an S.T.D. from the Pontifical John Paul II Institute in Rome. In addition to numerous articles, he has written and coauthored several books, including *La conoscenza morale: Linee di riflessione sul Commento di san Tommaso all'Etica Nicomachea* (Rome, 1987); *Moral: Tra crisi e rinnovamento* (Milan, 1993); *Corso di bioetica: Il Vangelo della vita* (Casale M., 1998); *Amor Conjugal y vocacion a la santidad* (with J. Laffitte; Santiago, 1997); *Sharing in Christ's Virtues; Cristo e il dinamismo dell'agire*

(Rome, 2001); *L'agire moral del cristiano* (Milan, 2002); *Per una cultura della famiglia: Il linguaggio dell'amore* (2006); *Walking in the Light of Love: The Foundations of Christian Morality* (2008); *Learning to Love: In the School of John Paul II and Benedict XVI* (2009); *The Epiphany of Love: Toward a Theological Understanding of Christian Action* (2010); and *Building a Culture of the Family: The Language of Love* (2011).

Daniel N. Robinson is a member of the philosophy faculty at Oxford University; distinguished professor, emeritus, at Georgetown University; and serves as visiting professor at the Institute for the Psychological Sciences. He served as president of two divisions of the American Psychological Association—the history of psychology and theoretical and philosophical psychology—and holds awards for Lifetime Achievement and Distinguished Contributions from the association. His areas of specialization include moral philosophy, philosophy of the mind, philosophy of psychology, legal philosophy, and the history of psychology. His sixteen books, more than thirty edited and published volumes, and numerous articles and lectures have addressed topics in the philosophy of sciences, intellectual history, philosophy of law, ethics, and the basic sciences. His most recent books include *Praise and Blame: Moral Realism and Its Applications* (Princeton University Press, 2002); *Consciousness and Mental Life* (Columbia University Press, 2008); *How Is Nature Possible? Kant's Project in the First Critique* (2012); *Personhood: What's in a Name? New Ideas in Psychology* (2012); and *Minds, Brains, and Brains in Vats* (2011).

Roger Scruton is a research scholar at Oxford University. He graduated from Cambridge University in 1965. He is an academic philosopher, writer, editor, and publisher who has served as professor of aesthetics at Birkbeck College, London, and as professor of philosophy and University Professor at Boston University. In addition to philosophical publications, he also writes fiction and political and cultural commentary. His most recent books include *The Face of God: The Gifford Lectures* (International Publishing Group, 2012); *Green Philosophy: How to Think Seriously about the Planet* (Atlantic Books, 2012); *The Uses of Pessimism and the Danger of False Hope* (Atlantic Books, 2010); *Beauty* (Oxford University Press, 2009); *Understand Music: Philosophy and Interpretation* (Continuum International Publishing Group, 2009); *Culture Counts: Faith and Feeling in a World Besieged* (Encounter Books, 2007); and *A Political Philosophy: Arguments for Conservatism* (Continuum, 2006).

INDEX OF NAMES

Adorno, Theodore, 77
Aquinas, St. Thomas, 6, 31–32, 36–37, 40, 51–55, 95, 101
Aristotle, 16, 98, 107–8, 135, 140
Arkes, Hadley, 10, 12, 95, 114
Augustine, St., 32

Barker, Ernest, 31
Barrett, H. Clark, 137
Bernard of Clairvaux, St., 68
Berto, Graziella, 75
Bird, Alexander, 136
Boethius, 31–32
Bork, Robert, 88–89
Boyle, Joseph, 43, 58–59, 62, 64
Bush, George W., 116, 118, 120

Caesar, Augustus, 29–30, 54
Calvin, John, 30
Casey, Richard Conway, 42–44, 56, 106
Castelli, Benedict, 71
Cates, Stephen, 90
Chesterton, G. K., 84–85, 91, 100, 104
Christine of Lorraine, 70
Cicero, 43
Cook, James, 131
Cooper, Samuel, 102
Cromwell, Thomas, 30

Darwin, Charles, 131
Director, Aaron, 90
Dostoyevsky, Fyodor, 99

Douglass, Frederick, 15
Dworkin, Ronald, 42

Eisgruber, Christopher L., 44, 56
El-Saadawi, Nawal, 129

Fabro, Cornelius, 74
Ferdinand of Spain, 30
Finnis, John, 4, 6–7, 32, 36, 39, 47, 52
Freud, Sigmund, 75
Fukuyama, Francis, 69

Gage, Thomas, 90
Galileo Galilei, 7, 70–71
Gelasius I, Pope, 30
Gelman, Susan, 137, 143
George, Robert P., 12–15, 47, 91, 103–4
Gierke, Otto, 31
Giussani, Luigi, 74
Granada, Daniel, 75
Grisez, Germain, 36, 38
Grotius, Hugo, 8, 73–74, 79, 83
Guardini, Romano, 76
Gurevich, Aaron, 33

Habermas, Jurgen, 61
Hamilton, Alexander, 10–11, 85, 95–97
Harre, Rom, 141
Heidegger, Martin, 71, 75
Henry VIII of England, 30
Heston, Charlton, 90
Hetata, Sherif, 129

Hilary, St., 33
Hobbes, Thomas, 11, 96–97
Horkheimer, Max, 77
Hume, David, 39

Ibn Khaldun, 27
Ibn Taymiyya, 26
Isabella of Spain, 30

Jefferson, Thomas, 93, 100
John Paul II, 12, 69, 104–6
Jonas, Hans, 72

Kant, Immanuel, 31, 33, 77, 104, 108
Ker, Ian, 39

Leiter, Brian, 41
Lewis, C. S., 68
Lincoln, Abraham, 95, 98, 100–101,
    107, 115
Locke, John, 12, 16, 97, 107, 132–35
Lund, Nelson, 90
Lustiger, Jean-Marie, 106–7

Macintyre, Alasdair, 82
Madison, James, 3, 10, 19, 91–92, 110
Malik, Charles, 18
Marshall, John, 87, 94
McLean, John, 99
Melina, Livio, 7–8, 75–76, 82
Mill, John Stuart, 106
Montesquieu, Baron de (Charles-Louis
    de Secondat), 15, 129–31
Moses, 105

Neier, Aryeh, 88
Newman, John Henry Cardinal, 22,
    39, 45

Nietzsche, Friedrich, 99
Noriega, José, 76, 82

Pannenberg, Wolfhart, 74
Pascal, Blaise, 9, 78–79
Pera, Benedetto, 79
Perez-Soba, Juan José, 75–76
Phalereus, Demetrius, 132
Piaget, Jean, 143
Plato, 68, 77, 82, 92–93, 135
Plutarch, 132

Qutb, Sayyid, 26

Ratzinger, Joseph, 70, 73, 79, 81
Rawls, John, 42, 45
Robinson, Daniel, vii, 15–16, 141
Robinson, John A. T., 46

Sager, Lawrence G., 44, 56
Schiavo, Terry, 129
Schindler, David L., 72, 81
Schmitz, Kenneth L., 80
Schwarzenegger, Arnold, 125
Scruton, Roger, 2–4, 18, 147
Sedgwick, Theodore, 85–86, 89
Spaemann, Robert, 76–77

Theseus, 132
Tocqueville, Alexis de, 110

Washington, George, 91, 93
Wenham, John, 46
Wilson, James, 10–11, 85, 94–97
Wolfe, Christopher, 47

INDEX OF SUBJECTS

abortion, 13–15, 23, 101–2, 113–17, 120
anticlericalism, 21
antimetaphysical, 8, 75
authority: religious, 29, 65; secular, 4,
    11, 17, 20–21, 27–28, 48, 53–54, 65, 93,
    109–10, 140

Bible: in counseling, 23–24
Bill of Rights, 10–11, 85–86, 94, 100
biotechnology, 7–8, 68–69, 117

Catholic Church, 53, 57, 100
civil unions, 126
cloning, 13–14, 113, 118–21, 127
coercion, 5–6, 49–52, 54–55, 58
common good, 5–6, 9, 13, 16, 45, 52, 55,
    78, 81–82
Communion, 25–26, 77, 81–82
Constitution of the United States, 2–3,
    10–11, 19–22, 24, 48, 56, 84–86, 89,
    91, 94–96, 100, 107
Creator, 7–9, 11–13, 39, 48, 69–70, 72–
    73, 78, 80–81, 91–92, 97, 100, 112

Darwinian revolution, 131
Dignitatis Humanae, 5–7, 49, 53–60
diversity, 15, 56, 130
Dred Scott case, 99, 139

essence, 16, 133–38, 140–41, 143
essentialism, 16, 134–43
existence of God: arguments for, 36

Fathers of the Church, 105
fetal farming, 14, 120
First Amendment, 2–5, 10, 18, 42, 48,
    85–91
first principles, 13, 109, 112
Founding Fathers, 3, 10, 13, 19–20, 24,
    85, 112
freedom, religious, 1–4, 18–28, 33–
    34, 42
free market, 13, 111

government, 11–16, 32–33, 58–65,
    86–90, 93–98, 109–12, 117, 121–27

human dignity, 2, 7, 9, 12, 15, 69,
    76, 81
human duties, 6–7, 15, 17, 26, 29, 31, 33,
    58, 65, 142–43
human nature, 7–8, 11–12, 15–16, 24,
    69, 131, 134–35, 138, 142
human rights, 1, 5–6, 10, 15, 17, 18, 43,
    45, 48, 56, 59–61, 69, 76, 78, 81, 127,
    140, 143

in vitro, 118–19
Islam, 3–4, 18–19, 21–22, 27–28, 57,
    61

Koran, 19, 28, 128

libertarianism, 110–11
Logos, 8–9, 73, 78, 80–83

marriage, 13–15, 113–14, 121–27
morality, 6–8, 48–50, 75–76, 110–11, 113
moral law, 11, 33, 91–94

"natural kinds," 136–38
natural law, 12–13, 32–33, 59–60, 101
negative duty, 6, 58, 62
"no establishment" clause, 19–24

person, 31–33, 53–54, 77, 81–82, 132–34, 139
pluralism, 15, 45, 129, 132
political philosophy, 5, 36, 42, 45, 48, 50
polyamory, 122
positive law, 10–11, 85, 92, 97–98
"posthuman world," 8, 68–69
privilege, 127, 140
pro-life movement, 114–18

reason, 9, 12, 31–32, 44–45, 73–76, 79–80, 83, 102–6

Regensburg Address, 6, 28, 50–51
religious sense, 12, 91, 107
revelation, 39–41, 65, 76–77, 101–3
revolution, principle of, 12, 97
Roman law, 30–32

same-sex "marriage," 15, 121–26
scientific rationality, 70–73
secularism, 2–4
ship of Theseus, 132
speech: freedom of, 86–90; rightful and wrongful use, 10, 26–28
state of nature, 95–96
stem-cell research, 14, 113, 119
subordination: of associations to state, 27
subsidiarity, 126

theocracy, 2–3, 21
Troglodytes, 130–31
"two swords" doctrine, 30

The John Henry Cardinal Newman Lectures
EDITED BY CRAIG STEVEN TITUS

1. *The Person and the Polis: Faith and Values within the Secular State* (2007)

2. *On Wings of Faith and Reason: The Christian Difference in Culture and Science* (2008)

3. *Christianity and the West: Interaction and Impact in Art and Culture* (2009)

4. *The Psychology of Character and Virtue* (2009)

5. *Philosophical Psychology* (2009)

Monograph Series

1. Fergus Kerr, *"Work on Oneself": Wittgenstein's Philosophical Psychology* (2008)

2. Kenneth L. Schmitz, *Person and Psyche* (2009)

3. Kevin L. Flannery, SJ, *Christian and Moral Action* (2012)

4. Benedict M. Ashley, OP, *Healing for Freedom: A Christian Perspective on Personhood and Psychotherapy* (2013)

God, Religion, and Civil Governance was designed in Minion Pro and composed by Kachergis Book Design of Pittsboro, North Carolina. It was printed on 60-pound Natures Natural Recycled and bound by McNaughton & Gunn of Saline, Michigan.